FROM HERE TO GREATER HAPPINESS

OR HOW TO CHANGE YOUR LIFE— FOR GOOD!

BY JOEL MARIE TEUTSCH
CHAMPION K. TEUTSCH, PH.D.

REVISED – NEW – ENLARGED EDITION
OF THE THE BEST-SELLING *FROM HERE TO HAPPINESS*

PRICE/STERN/SLOAN
Publishers, Inc., Los Angeles

Contents
PART I
UNDERSTAND YOUR CONSCIOUSNESS !

Contents (Cont'd.)

PART II

RAISE YOUR CONSCIOUSNESS !

ACKNOWLEDGEMENT

No man can claim sole authorship of his works. For he is the beneficiary of all who preceded, taught, stimulated and collaborated with him. Because I was awakened and guided to the unique understanding and application of all knowledge contained in this publication by my beloved wife and teacher, Joel Marie Teutsch, I gratefully acknowledge her as my co-author. It was she who contributed what sets our methodology apart from others: insight into the dynamics of SSP (suprasensory perception) and the spirit — not as a religious but scientific reality. Her selflessness and personal sacrifices, including verified healings, made possible the results that inaugurated the Consciousness Revolution and other developments beneficial to the progress of mankind.

Also gratefully acknowledged is the assistance of those who, through their research, experience, sacrifice, and permission to mention or quote their writings or experiences, made possible the publication of this book.

Special thanks are expressed to our loyal clients, students, colleagues and friends throughout the world who trusted, used, and verified the validity of the principles discussed by us.

C. K. T.

Los Angeles, California

FOREWORD

The purpose of this revised and enlarged edition is to give the reader a more thorough, yet practical understanding of the scientific principles discovered and used by us in our private practice. By now, at least some of them have been validated by other authors, professionals and academicians. Our assertions about traffic safety were splendidly confirmed by the Safety Research and Education Project at Columbia University. According to written and oral reports, probably millions were enabled to achieve better results in marriage, occupation and daily life.

Part I, based upon our original paper, "The Effect of Consciousness on Human Behavior and Mechanical Performance," dated October 7, 1959, and our Teutsch IDEAL (individualized-directive-explanatory-action-log) Method — abbreviated to TIM, has been updated and expanded. Instead of stressing the race for space, we have added our comprehensive conclusions. Also included is a brief discussion of Gene-physics (Mental Genetics and Human Physics), as developed, used and described by us in scientific papers we presented at international symposia. In response to widespread demands, four new practical chapters have been added to Part II.

These modifications, we feel, justify our and our publishers' confidence that this volume will become even more popular and useful than the first one.

J. M. T.
C. K. T.

INTRODUCTION

Man has discovered most of the laws governing his physical environment. He has learned to walk the moon, split the atom, and understand at least a part of the genetic code. He has designed and built machines, complex devices, structures and electro-mechanical systems for every conceivable purpose. He can foretell their performance with fair accuracy.

Thanks to science and engineering, life on earth has become progressively more "controllable" — in a non-political sense. Many factors of uncertainty, which made it appear that the individual was at the mercy of forces beyond his reach, have been reduced or eliminated.

For example, current design practices, safety codes and inspection requirements protect buildings against collapse, fire, earthquake and other hazards.

Traffic by land, sea and air moves on schedule with relatively little chance of accident.

Similar improvements benefit mankind in medicine and sanitation, agriculture and food technology, the manufacture of machinery, clothing and equipment, and in dozens of other areas.

The Chance Factor in Human Behavior:

Only one large field has remained a baffling mystery, at least to the majority of mankind. Human behavior and experience — whether on the singular, group or universal level — appear to be subject to chance factors. Although many people have been successfully influenced by education, psychotherapy, advertising and media, interpersonal relations seem to be unpredictable to a frustrating degree.

The executive in charge of 15,000 employees cannot get his wife to see his side of his argument or even convince his son to get a haircut. His mate, on the other hand, commands the love and cooperation of the members of her club, but is unable to get her husband to listen to her.

The President of the United States, though Commander-in-Chief of the Army, Navy, and Air Force and probably the most powerful man on earth, is helpless against a bullet fired from a mail-order rifle.

Human Behavior - Predictable:

In our first paper and publication preceding this revised edition, we explored some of these phenomena. In our subsequent papers on Human Physics* and on Mental Genetics**, we presented our theory that *all human behavior and experience is predictable and therefore, if desired, alterable in accordance with the same laws that govern rocketry and the orbit of the planets around the stars.*

We established transformations of these laws into their equivalents in application to man. (I defined the international unit of consciousness as 1 joel and its physical symbol as the DNA — deoxyribonucleic acid — in the cell nucleus. C.K.T.)

Our research on thousands upon thousands of cases has shown the validity of these transformations on the singular, collective and universal scale. As a result, it has been possible for us to formulate rules for achieving desirable objectives. Among these are peace, prosperity, freedom from unfavorable conditions, and success for the individual, the group (ranging from two-member families to giant corporations), the nation and the world.

Victimology: An Effect of Consciousness, Interpersonal Dynamics and Human Physics, presented at the First International Symposium on Victimology in Jerusalem, Israel, on September 4, 1973; later published in the *International Journal of Criminology and Penology*, December, 1974, and *Lexington Books*, Lexington, Massachusetts, 1974.

**Criminality As A Function of Mental Genetics*, presented at the First International Symposium on Criminology in Sao Paulo, Brazil, on August 8, 1974; later published in the annals of the Oscar Freire Institute, Sao Paulo, 1975.

These rules, we have shown, could be tremendously useful to industry and government, with much waste of time, money, and manpower eliminated by application of our findings to the solution of vexing social, economic and international problems. On a larger scale, the future of all mankind could be secured.

Our discoveries took place not in the physical world — the lowest dimension of earthly existence, the realm of the visible, audible, tangible and directly measurable — but, at least some of them in the second dimension, the invisible and immense region of mind.

Actuality of Life:

This elementary document does not purport to be a blueprint for utopia. Neither is it concerned with metaphysical or mystical speculations. Starting with already known phenomena, some confirmed by scientific research under carefully controlled conditions, we proceed to our principal laboratory: the infinitely diversified, yet irrefutable, actuality of life, as mirrored in our long-time private practice. We also explain principles for understanding and for proving certain behavior patterns which we have found to work time after time, often after other approaches had failed to produce any desired results.

Our initial, highly tenuous hypotheses eventually became theories which, as they proved effective in case after case, we translated into the laws included in the succeeding chapters and, particularly, the already mentioned scientific papers.

In the future, we plan to present applications of our unique Gene-physics concepts to every field of human endeavor. As always, our emphasis will be on clarity, simplicity and unity.

All cases mentioned in this book — including those involving cancer and other serious diseases — are real. Names, dates and other details are available to qualified inquirers.* Many have been verified by physicians and attorneys.

Our motive is not — and has never been — to establish and perpetuate a secret monopoly. On the contrary, we continually renew our offer to explain in full detail our methodology and to demonstrate its effectiveness before academic, professional or other bodies anywhere.

It is our sincere hope that those interested in reducing fear, ignorance, war, accident, failure, frustration, and the prohibitive cost of needless medication and hospitalization will accept it.

C. K. T.

*NOTICE: To safeguard the privacy of individuals discussed in our examples, names have been deleted from this book. These names are on file in our Century City office: suite 1785, 1900 Avenue of the Stars, Los Angeles, California 90067.

PART I

UNDERSTAND YOUR CONSCIOUSNESS

A. FUNCTIONS OF MIND

1. NATURE

One does not have to know anything about gravity to be subject to the law governing this important force. By the same token, no man has ever seen electricity, but we all are using it in different ways. The same goes for the laws of mind. Although we may be unaware of their existence, we are nevertheless affected by them every second of our lives.

Mind, as we call or know it, cannot be seen. But it does not require much reflection to realize that it is a potent, ever-present reality. For a long time, the brain was considered to be the seat of our mind, essential for our survival as an intelligent being. Recent evidence has destroyed this belief. The reasoning and acting ability of a few war victims deprived of one or both cerebral hemispheres was found to be unimpaired. As a result, we are forced to conclude that *the mind is our invisible control center*, with the brain merely acting as its physical agent and symbol.

This is by no means intended to imply that the brain is unnecessary. What it does prove, however, is that the brain is controlled by mind. Mind, being greater than the brain, can under certain conditions take over and perform the functions of the brain, in addition to its own.

Here is a splendid example. A hemispherectomy — the surgical removal of half the human brain — left a 9-year-old boy who suffered from a massive tumor almost normal. Before the operation at Fresno's Valley Children's Hospital, in November, 1967, Tony Salas of Porterville, California, suffered painful headaches, impaired vision and could not walk by himself due to a 50% to 75% paralysis of his left arm and leg.

"The fact that the mind rules the body is the most fundamental fact we know about the process of life." This is no layman's generalization. It was the considered view of the late Dr. Franz Alexander, director of the Psychiatric and Psychosomatic Research Institute at Mt. Sinai Hospital in Los Angeles. "Our emotions," he continued, "are accompanied by physiological changes; fear, by palpitation of the heart; anger, by increased heart activity, elevation of blood pressure, by changes in carbohydrate metabolism."

Anger, it should be noted parenthetically, may be a mere cover for fear of embarrassment, insecurity, harm and other causes.

Clearly, emotions cause motions in the form of definite thoughts, beliefs, or actions, while the physiological changes are mere secondary effects. Of course, externally and internally noticeable physiological changes in turn set off emotional reactions which merely serve to intensify the already induced physical condition.

Along the same lines, a team of researchers (Drs. Eliot Corday, Sanford Rothenberg and David M. Irving of Los Angeles' Cedars of Lebanon Hospital) have furnished scientific proof that anger or fear can cause a stroke. Others (Drs. Edward J. Koller, Donald T. Fullerton and Alex B. Caldwell of U.C.L.A.'s Neuropsychiatric Institute) ascribed ulcerative colitis to emotional factors. On

November 13, 1965*, we claimed that fear, hate and guilt underlie most forms of cancer. Similar reports followed (by Dr. George F. Solomon, associate professor of clinical psychiatry at Stanford University School of Medicine, and Dr. Claus Bahnson, director of the Department of Behavioral Sciences in Pennsylvania, on April 5, 1971). They indicated that "nice guys" may well be more prone to becoming cancer victims than persons who are openly hostile. In subsequent years, emotions were held responsible by various researchers for arthritis, asthma, tuberculosis, big hives, and the common cold. We encountered the latter condition in cases of confusion.

2. APPLICATIONS

Remarkable physical reactions can be induced by beliefs which we accept voluntarily or involuntarily because of persuasion, suggestion, and experience. For example, through hypnosis, an intensive form of suggestion, it is possible to cause a subject in a perfectly cold room to perspire and shed his coat by convincing his mind that he is in the Sahara Desert.

In a more constructive application of the same principle, many clinics treat warts purely psychologically with astonishing success. Dr. J. B. Rhine** reports the treatment of burns by suggestion. According to competent observers, in many cases blistering is avoided.

Also, while observers are watching, blisters can be made to appear without the external application of heat and to disappear in the absence of medication by influencing the mind through intense suggestion.

---

*"Cancer' and Emotions." An address before the first state convention of the International Association of Cancer Victims and Friends at the Ambassador Hotel, Los Angeles, later published in the December, 1965, issue of the *Cancer News Journal.*

**New World of the Mind*, by J. B. Rhine, New York: William Sloane Associates, 1953; p. 37

Similarly, frigidity in women, overweight, personality disorders, and addiction to alcohol and narcotics can be removed.

We can observe the same principle in action on other occasions. The very thought of a cold drink usually stimulates a thirsty person. Mental activity of this sort also may apply to food, sex, and other areas of interest. In such cases, thought induces reactions in the body or actions by the body. As a rule, advertising in the media enlists the visual or auditory sense to achieve the identical result.

A well-known experiment conducted at a large Midwestern University some time ago deserves mention here. Several students, known for their inability to sleep after drinking coffee, were given, shortly before their bedtime, milk enriched with caffein extracted from coffee which was fed subsequently to an identical number of other students with the same anti-coffee bias. The first group, unaware of the caffein content of the milk, promptly went into a deep, undisturbed sleep, while the second group remained awake for hours, tossing fitfully in their dormitory beds.

An interesting and pertinent industrial experiment was made by a giant industrial organization several years ago. A group of assemblers had complained about the poor lighting in a section of the plant. An electrician removed the objectionable neon tubing from the ceiling fixtures in plain view of the workers. He promised to install, during the lunch period, new tubes he had piled neatly on a bench under the watchful eyes of the dissatisfied employees. In their absence, the electrician removed the unused tubes from the room and put the old ones back into their sockets. When the workers returned, believing their complaint had been heeded by the management, they expressed their pleasure with the "new" lights. Their grumbling ceased. Absenteeism and terminations diminished appreciably. Nothing was changed except the belief of a few disgruntled people.

Belief:

To verify the theory that *belief,* not external factors, *is responsible for physical healing,* a group of doctors at the medical school of a famous West Coast University conducted a compelling experiment. Six patients suffering from cancer of the skin were conditioned to expect good results from X-ray treatments. Three patients, instead of receiving these treatments, were wheeled into a room containing the necessary apparatus which was never turned on. The diseased portions of their body were exposed to the inactive equipment; the rest was covered with the customary protective clothing. Doctors and nurses acted around these patients as if actual X-ray treatments were being given. These patients, fully convinced that they had been treated as outlined, were healed without the usual tissue deterioration. Of the rest, one recovered, while two made no progress. All three, however, suffered the undesirable tissue effect. They had been told that this would occur and expected it.

Suddenly, previously unexplained occurrences become understandable. We may also be able to clear the names of several sincere citizens condemned as cancer quacks by a California legislative committee in Sacramento. They claimed to have cured many patients, some of whom testified in moving language that their lives were saved by "quack" therapy after they failed to respond to regular medical treatment. Officers of the American Medical Association, on the other hand, introduced evidence that none of the cases under their observation were healed by the unorthodox methods. The legislators, the press, and most of the public concluded, quite understandably, that the accused were guilty of fraud. Their witnesses were called "gullible dupes." On the basis of our discussion it is now possible to suppose that the so-called quacks and their enthusiastic supporters trusted fully in the unorthodox methods, while the medical doctors did not. Each got exactly what he believed.

Mental Factors:

We ascribe our own successes with individuals suffering from supposedly incurable conditions to mental rather than physical factors. We are neither physicians nor psychiatrists. Yet, we have seen total, rapid and permanent remissions in many cases.

One was a 35-year-old New York salesman who had suffered two myocardiac infractions (heart attacks), given up his job, ceased all sexual activity with his wife and began to prepare for death upon the advice of doctors at New York City's Bellevue Hospital and the U.C.L.A. Medical Center.

Another was a 29-year-old Wichita, Kansas housewife who had not responded to years of treatment, including surgery, for Hodgkins' disease by her personal physician or the National Institute of Health at Bethesda Naval Hospital in Maryland.

A third example pertains to a desperate couple who had, for 17 years, visited physicians and psychiatrists, including V.A. specialists, all over the country, because of a condition diagnosed as colitis, migraine headaches, schizophrenia and paranoidal delusions. A fourth was a 15-year-old Canoga Park, California high-school girl whose entire body was covered with psoriasis.

Still another case was that of a 36-year-old executive secretary who had been diagnosed as a catatonic schizophrenic but had not responded to two years of treatment by physicians and psychiatrists at Gateways Psychiatric Hospital in Los Angeles.

In each of these cases, our Teutsch IDEAL (individualized-directive-explanatory-action-log) Method — abbreviated to TIM — brought almost instant insight and relief by changing the responsible mental factors.

Example:

Dr. Carl Simonton of Fort Worth, Texas, specializes in cancer therapy. In an address on "New Dimensions of Healing" presented by the Academy of Parapsychology and Medicine and Spiritual Frontiers Fellowship in Chicago, on January 4, 1974, he said he uses mind-over-matter techniques in healing his patients.

A typical case demonstrating the effect of belief on physical results is that of Benjamin Brown, 20. He was riding a rapid transit car to his job as a cook at a San Leandro, California restaurant on June 7, 1973. A man rushed up shouting, "Doctor, doctor, come quick!" Brown, who was wearing a white coat, protested: "Wait a minute, I'm no doctor, I'm a . . . "

"No time for explanations," the man interrupted. "A little girl is sick in the next car."

"What could I do?" Brown said later. He followed the man and saw a girl about six years old on the floor of the car. Her mother was leaning over her, crying for help. Again Brown tried to explain he was a cook, but all the mother said was, "Please, doctor, help her."

Brown knelt down and began mouth-to-mouth resuscitation he had learned in a high-school first-aid course.

"I've never been so nervous," said Brown. "I was even shaking. I was blowing and hoping."

The little girl revived and snuggled into the arms of her mother, who barely had time to thank Brown before he left the train to go to work. He probably did not realize that primarily responsible for his success was the confidence that the child, the mother and those watching had placed in him.

3. EFFECT OF BELIEF

Mind, it is quite obvious by now, is a potent instrument. It *produces for us results not according to the facts but according to our belief.* Ignorance, in other words, can be bliss.

The rural natives of Mexico or Eskimo tribes far removed from civilization, for instance, subsist on highly monotonous diets which, according to nutritionists, should induce disease and debility. Instead, these "primitive" people enjoy perfect health; baldness, tooth decay, and skin disorders are unknown to them. After they are taught about lack of vitamins and minerals, however, they start exhibiting all the deficiencies familiar to the experts.

Many examples illustrate the effect of belief about diet. Some people will become slim and trim because they count calories. Others, convinced that calories don't count, will get the same results. Still others thrive on an all-protein diet. A fourth group swears that carbohydrates alone will burn fat off their bodies. According to certain gurus, only raw vegetables will do the trick. Others counsel the public to simply eat less of everything. By contrast, there are those who insist that health food is essential for well-being or survival. Similar claims are made for vitamin pills, other special pills or exercise.

In the final analysis, what matters is not what man puts into his body but what he tells it to do for him. Like Britain's Winston Churchill, who "only" lived to be 94, many centenarians ascribe their achievement to brandy, cigars and eating to their heart's content. Others credit abstinence and moderation for their longevity.

We all know of people who, while inebriated, survived car crashes which would have been fatal to people in command of their faculties.

In 1959, two drunkards in the French town of Vienne opened what they thought was a door to the street. Actually it was the window of a room four stories up. With a gay song on their lips, they marched out arm in arm — over the sill to the street below. A beat policeman, hearing the thuds and rushing to help, was dumbfounded to watch them career away, still singing and obviously in tip-top condition. "We missed our step," they explained. These lucky people just did not know they were in danger.

To show the effect of contrasting beliefs, a certain newspaper item is pertinent. On July 7, 1959, a two-year-old Palos Verdes, California child was happily playing in his garden pen with an object that to his mother, in the nearby kitchen, appeared like a long piece of hose. After about 30 minutes, the mother decided to get a closer look from the window. To her horror, she realized the "hose" was a rattlesnake. She screamed a loud warning but, according to the article, it was "too late." The child was badly injured. In truth, he was not in danger because he did not know that his playmate was dangerous. The implication is obvious that the mother's positive belief that the snake would bite caused the almost fatal tragedy. Had the mother gone about her business, the snake in all likelihood eventually would have left its little playmate alone by slithering peacefully from the scene.

According to the belief of most people, including champion weight-lifters, a 126-pound middle-aged woman cannot move a 3600-pound load. Yet this is precisely what a Tampa, Florida woman did on April 25, 1960, when her 16-year-old son was pinned under a station wagon because of a slipped jack. In what she described as "virtual hysteria," she was oblivious of all the laws of physics when she saw her son in danger. She grabbed a bumper of the car, lifted with all her might, released her son, and was in good condition except for several cracked vertebrae.

And this was no isolated occurrence. On May 9, 1968, 20-year-old Janet K. Stone, 5'5" and weighing 110 pounds, saved her father's life by "overpowering" a 1500-pound car which had fallen atop him when the jack apparently slipped. In an upsurge of incredible strength, she lifted the three-quarter-ton car, pulled Robert H. Stone aside, carried him to her car, and drove to the nearest hospital in Covina, California.

B. INDIVIDUAL CONSCIOUSNESS

1. DEFINITIONS

By way of analogy, mind may be likened to an invisible programmer who knows all the rules pertaining to any given specific human activity, such as walking, typing, driving, piloting a plane or playing tennis. Mind imprints upon the brain, which acts like a highly efficient computer, whatever knowledge the individual may require at any given moment. For instance, the mind may make a baby conscious of the possibility of walking by causing it to observe others who move about on their feet. But the brain will not know that the little tyke can walk until he has successfully done so.

The conscious level of our being, similar to the tip of an iceberg protruding out of the ocean, contains the small amount of knowledge within range of our immediate awareness. The subconscious, or submerged part, is included in our brain which may be compared to a subjective or personal hall of records containing all we ever learned, experienced, did, felt, and thought. What we call mind also has an unconscious level that is filled with the total body of knowledge or events outside our own individual range of experience.

As soon as the brain has learned whatever the mind has entrusted to its care, the mind will make us conscious of new activities necessary for our progress. After we have mastered the art of walking, for example, we will become aware of running. It can thus be stated that, thanks to the subconscious, *our past is ever with us, being constantly modified by the present,* or conscious level of our mind, *to produce our future into being.*

Subconscious Influence:

Instead of being isolated and apart from us, the subconscious and unconscious constantly influence our thinking and behavior. Their interaction with the conscious creates what may be fittingly called our *consciousness, the sum-total of our beliefs, attitudes, feelings, thoughts, acts, ideas, experiences.* Conversely, conscious learning — especially through repetition — steadily filters into the subconscious and from there into the unlimited unconscious.

As a result, we can liken mind to a unified electrical field with energy characteristics that are unique for the applicable activity. This field contains as many cells or human individuals, objects and other factors as belong to it by virtue of concept, understanding, action and experience. Though hundreds of thousands of pilots may be in the appropriate mind, a collective, the brain record of each differs, often drastically, because of each individual's unique interpretation of his knowledge and experience as a pilot.

2. CONSCIOUSNESS AS CAUSE

Another vital function of *mind is as the sender and receiver of electrical emanations or thought waves.* Thought is power. This is no mere platitude. Physically measurable in terms of one or two microvolts, it differs from the output of a giant broadcasting station only in magnitude. Yet, its capability is infinitely greater. For no radio station, no house, no car, no visible object at all can come into being without thought. The invisible thinking process precedes the emergence of the tangible result.

The strong belief by Thomas A. Edison, despite universal scepticism, in the possibility of using electricity for lighting, produced the bulb which revolution-ized life on this planet for all time to be. Similarly, the Wright brothers made history at Kitty Hawk, after learned men the world over had proved "conclusively" the impossibility of flying in machines heavier than air. The Wrights, fortunately, never listened to these experts.

The visible end product, in spite of all contributory physical effort, is merely the crystallization of the original consciousness and, secondarily, the thought that produced it into being. This apparent simplification actually is scientific truth. For example, photographs taken at Oxford University of a person's scalp during intensive concentration on a knife clearly showed the imaged object, down to minute details, as if suspended in the air slightly above the head of the thinker. Specialized studies have proved that brain or thought waves consist of the same infinitesimal small light or radiation particles found in the atom. All matter, regardless of its apparent solidity, is composed of atoms that, in turn, consist of protons around which electrons are spinning constantly. As a result, matter must be regarded as a fluid in static vibration. Thought is an effect of consciousness. Therefore, in the final analysis, *consciousness and matter are the same* because they have the same basic components.

Lincoln Barnett* summarizes the view of philosophers and scientists from the ancient Greek Democritus to Albert Einstein that " . . . the whole objective universe of matter and energy, atoms and stars, does not exist except as a construction of consciousness, an edifice of symbols shaped by the senses of man."

The original light bulb was, in a very real sense, a manifestation of Edison's consciousness. More precisely, it was a projection outward, into the environment, of an inner belief. As soon as his contemporaries saw or learned of his invention, thus becoming conscious of it, electric light became widely used. Again, the invisible consciousness preceded the visible result. Thanks to the many new applications and the general acceptance of this new power, we all are now electricity-conscious.

Consciousness, we now see clearly, *is the internal antecedent to external manifestation or expression.* Using the Edison example, the physical expression of individual consciousness serves, in turn, as stimulus for changing the consciousness of the group and then of the mass, by a process we may call cultural cross-pollination, through the medium of learning.

3. LEARNING

Our consciousness is shaped by what we know. In turn, all our knowledge stems from learning of one or more of the following kinds:

a. Study (concentration and deliberation, as at school)
b. Observation (unconscious observation and imitation)
c. Hearing
d. Feeling
e. Other Processes

---

* *The Universe and Dr. Einstein,* by L. K. Barnett, New York: William Sloane Associates, Inc., 1957; p. 11.

This learning is impressed by our mind on its physical instrument, the brain, in a form resembling the grooves on a record. The predominant grooves are then played over and over again.

Even learning of short duration alters the brain record permanently. Our long-standing contentions on this point were confirmed in 1966, through an experiment by Dr. Evelyn Lee-Teng at the California Institute of Technology. It was found that learning of a specific sort had become firmly established in 2000 chicks only thirty seconds after their exposure to a certain stimulus.

When we learn to type, for example, we have to start by understanding and remembering consciously the location and function of the many keys on the typewriter. Again, through conscious effort, we learn whatever system we want to use. In the beginning, we type slowly and jerkily, making frequent mistakes. After some practice, as our coordination improves, we gain confidence. Eventually, we do not have to think any more where to place our fingers. We type smoothly and rhythmically. What we have learned consciously has filtered into our subconscious which now repeats and applies the newly acquired knowledge automatically.

Once we learn something, we have learned it forever, even though we may not use it or have consciously forgotten it. After we have learned to accept as true an absolute premise, e.g., that we gain weight through eating, our agreement with identical information will be subconscious or automatic, while we become consciously aware of knowledge to the contrary and disagree.

Early learning penetrates deeper than more recent learning. For instance, the habit of communicating in one's native tongue makes difficult the mastery of a foreign language. Even after acquiring proficiency in a new language, one tends to revert to the more familiar mother tongue when the conscious guard is down.

4. ENVIRONMENT AS EFFECT

By analogy, the subconscious reproduces environmental conditions and experiences with amazing fidelity. This explains why our childhood has a critical bearing on what we are and do in later life. Even subsequent learning can have far-reaching consequences.

Through study, observation, and hearing, for example, many doctors become extremely conscious of certain diseases. Their mind, like a camera, has taken so many pictures of the nature, symptoms, and effects of these conditions that their subconscious finally reproduces them with utmost fidelity in their own bodies.

The following cases* deserve special mention here.

Jeffrey A. Gottlieb, 35, chief of chemotherapy service at the University of Texas Cancer Center, died on July 9, 1975, after a struggle with the disease for which he had been seeking a cure.

Dr. Peter F. Salisbury, 51, noted Los Angeles heart and kidney researcher, died November 5, 1964, of a heart attack.

Vivian Sturgeon, who was busy helping women who came to the local Henson Memorial Cancer Society for free cancer detection examinations, was found to have a malignancy on July 15, 1975. She had a modified radical mastectomy. "I never thought it would happen to me," she admitted, adding, "I certainly did not order cancer." (Consciously, at least, we add.)

*Reported by the *Los Angeles Times* one day after the indicated death dates.

At the 1963 meeting of the American Medical Association in Atlantic City, Dr. Thomas M. Peery, chief of pathology at George Washington University School of Medicine, set up a special laboratory which gave free examinations to 1,504 of the attending physicians. *About four out of five showed some abnormality in their blood or urine.* Many had more than one abnormal finding.

We are convinced that these and countless other examples lend dramatic proof to the belief that mental rather than physical contagion was involved.

Dr. Sherwyn M. Woods, Joseph M. Natterson and Jerome Silverman of the USC Medical School reported on August 12, 1965, that 26 out of 33 senior medical students chosen at random suffered from MSD — "Medical Student Disease." The diseases ranged from cancer, tuberculosis, heart disease and kidney ailments to psychiatric disorders.

The same principle applies to the couvade (French word meaning to cover, or to hatch), the tendency for a husband to suffer the symptoms of pregnancy experienced by his wife. In some parts of France and South America, when a woman is confined, her spouse takes to his bed and is visited and congratulated by the neighbors — as if he had the baby! A British study* showed that one in nine husbands gets some of these sympathetic symptoms. Dr. Arthur Coleman, a California psychiatrist, says today a number of obstetricians are helping husbands to stay close to their wives in sympathy and affection during pregnancy. In one Boston study, 80 of 200 men with pregnant wives developed pregnancy symptoms — morning sickness, abnormal cravings for food, an increasingly prominent pot belly.

State of Consciousness Expressed:

The focused-upon conditions may not show up in the body of a doctor, nurse, social worker or sympathetic layman. Instead, they may make their appear-

Today's Health, September, 1966

ance, on a basis modified by various factors, in a family member or members of the one involved with these conditions on a professional or human-interest basis. This is a graphic example of what we have learned to call a projective expression of a state of consciousness.

The same principle is graphically illustrated by the case of a widow, reported by Dr. Walter Alvarez of Mayo Clinic fame. He expressed his admiration for this woman who had been in a mental hospital, apparently hopelessly afflicted with a severe depression. According to Alvarez, the psychiatrists could do little for her. Then her husband died suddenly. The woman got out of bed, put on her clothes, and said, "Let me out." First, she took care of her five children. Then she got an executive position in a large company. "She has done wonderfully well in her work," Alvarez reported, and he ascribed her recovery to will power.

We disagree. Her husband's death, we contend, stopped the undesirable mental or conceptual activity which, we feel, had influenced her. As a result she could return to her normal, effective state.

Similar causes, we assert, underlie psychiatric disorders in 60 physicians' wives who were admitted to a private psychiatric hospital, according to a report by Dr. James L. Evans of the Institute of Living, Hartford, Connecticut, published in the December, 1965 issue of the *American Journal of Psychiatry*.

The principle applicable here is the mental equivalent to that discovered in the case of "Typhoid Mary." This turn-of-the-century domestic never came down with the disease herself. But in every household in which she worked, there were victims.

Learning of a more constructive kind can also influence our consciousness strongly. Many a little girl, all dolled up in her mother's finery, pranced in front of the mirror feeling so vividly like a beauty queen that, years later, she actually became one. A striking case in point is Tawny Elaine Godin, 18, who was crowned Miss America on September 6, 1975. Asked how it felt to take the long walk to accept her crown, she candidly admitted to be quite familiar in this role. "I have practiced it ever since I was five," she said.

Actors are frequently assigned roles conforming to their true life experience. Sometimes their subconscious may compel them to take up, offstage, the profession or habit pattern of a character they liked and portrayed realistically for a period of time. It may even impel their return from retirement.

By unconscious observation and associated learning, people become aware of sickness, poverty, failure, argument, loneliness, crime, accident, or futility. Their subconscious, suffused with this learning, as a rule will create identical conditions in their adult life. In the same manner, one may pattern oneself after a domineering father, a nagging mother, a rebellious brother. The subconscious mind is impartial. It re-creates what man has become conscious of. One person may focus on the weaknesses of another so strongly that he displays them himself, to his dismay, years later. By similar means, people learn to age, wear glasses, become deaf, lose their teeth, grow fat. Contrary to popular opinion, the belief — or, actually, the conviction — that age and its symptoms are inevitable must precede those results which are mere physical effects.

These facts teach us valuable lessons. Intelligent, systematic effort can benefit us. It could truly bring into being a generation of healthy, youthful, confident, successful and happy men and women.

On the other hand, one may become conscious of undesirable behavior in others. Someone's nagging, teasing, insulting or violence will impress itself so strongly on people's subconscious that others in the future may behave toward him in similar fashion, although he has consciously forgotten the persons, times and places involved in the early experiences.

It is worth noting that we become painfully aware of unpleasant conditions and behavior while we take for granted our states of apparent fulfillment. Something greater than our conscious self seems to demand that we rid ourselves of what irritates or obstructs us. This fact reveals a great truth:

Good is natural. All else is unnatural.

This fact explains a common phenomenon. After people, including scoundrels and criminals, die, most survivors tend to remember only their noble qualities and deeds. The reason is simple. The individual's undesirable concepts about himself/herself and others have vanished, only to be replaced with "good" concepts, untarnished by worldly conditioning or misconception.

Repetition:

In the third kind of learning mentioned, every word to which we are exposed, even though we do not consciously hear it, enters our consciousness, cutting a groove into the ever-playing record. With repetition, the groove deepens to produce its analogous external result.

A parent's statement to a child that he is no good may produce a bad-consciousness with all its consequences in the form of such undesirable feelings and actions as are encountered in juvenile delinquency.

Years later, teachers, judges, spouses, employers of the "evil" person may blame him for his hostile attitude and behavior. In many cases, he himself will agree with them. But it was the father who with his critical words set into motion the unfortunate chain of circumstances. *Words are like seeds falling on fertile ground —* our brain. And what is sown there, regardless of our age, we must reap sooner or later in the form of three-dimensional, technicolored results.

The mother of an adolescent killed in a car crash may scream, "If he had only listened to me!" Sympathetic onlookers are bound to agree with her unless they realize, as we do, that it was her constantly reiterated warnings of the dangers of driving which helped to produce a consciousness, an unconscious expectation, of accidents. On the other hand, the family of a crash victim may blame the other driver for his carelessness without suspecting that it was their loved one's consciousness, plus their own, which was, at least in part, responsible. Of course, the other driver contributed to the calamity through his consciousness and that of those close to him.

Parent Conditioning:

A boy conditioned by his parents not to trust a living soul is likely to encounter one disillusioning experience after another. "Aha," he will say at last, "my parents were right. The world is full of crooks." Each crook, however, is merely an effect, while his victim's consciousness is a cause. To be sure, the evildoer has a disposition or desire to harm another. But it takes a belief in, or fear of, the existence of men like him to bring into being the expected wrong.

By the same token, a doctor removing a tumor is concerned only with an effect. The cause is the victim's belief in cancer or its power to kill, a great hate, frustration, or other emotional condition. The effect will recur, either as another tumor or another disease, unless the cause is cleared up.

Probably no other learning process influences the human individual more profoundly than that which pertains to his feelings. Like most forms of learning, this one has its start early in life. A child usually feels very good about such a natural act as fondling his genitals. His parents may teach him to regard that same act as bad. By the process of stimulus generalization, he will learn to associate the resulting feelings of guilt or wrong with feeling good and reproduce them every time he has a pleasant emotional state. The understandable confusion resulting from this interaction between two basically antagonistic forms of interpretation is an important cause of mental illness.

Learning, we have observed, is also transmitted by other means. When a person makes a discovery or invention, he taps a source of information not contained in any library or other person's brain record. Apparently he is in extrasensory contact with the intelligence controlling man's affairs.

Everything we perceive in our environment is an external effect of an internal or invisible cause. In turn, every external effect serves as a cause for subsequent internal changes in us. Thus we can observe here a perfect interaction between man and his outer world.

Power of the Subconscious:

One of our clients, a 6'4" salesman, provides an excellent example of the power of the subconscious to influence human behavior. He had an excellent ability to relate to all people on a social basis. But whenever it came to asking for their signature or money, he perspired heavily and suffered severe palpitations. As a child, we found, he had been beaten twice when he asked his powerful father for money to go to the movies.

We found that the same principle applies to animals. Lolita, a powerful four-year-old black leopard, had no fear of humans or other animals. But when a certain little mutt came near her cage, she would cower in fright. Puzzled zoo-keepers asked us for an explanation. We gave it readily. When the big cat was a three-week-old cub, the little dog had beaten her up, almost killing her. In her subconscious mind, he still could do it.

Pit ponies, after pulling circular pumps in Welsh coal mines for 17 years, are put to pasture. Instead of walking straight ahead, they continue to move along the familiar curved orbital path.

5. LIFE PATTERNS

To summarize, *thought accumulates into a personal belief — and ultimately conviction — which*, after suffusing our subconscious, *dominates our life*, including our attitudes, actions, experiences, environment, according to a definite, clearly discernible pattern. This pattern may be positive and produce success, health, happiness, and other desirable effects with repetitive monotony. The man of whom people say, "Everything he touches turns to gold," obviously is success- or money-conscious, and not fortunate in the commonly used sense.

On a few television shows, a young girl known for her good luck since early childhood was pitted against a professional Las Vegas gambler in several games picked by him. Due to her amazing mental attitude, she won every time with ease. The man, by comparison, was not nearly as confident in his ability to prevail. Nothing succeeds like success-consciousness.

The 6th Sense:

Successful businessmen seem to be gifted with a sixth sense, an intuitive ability to foresee the future and make the tough, unexpected decisions that pay off handsomely. The fact that intuition does pay off was reported by E. Douglas Dean, research associate at the Newark College of Engineering, to the American Association for the Advancement of Science.* In a test of 67 high executives, mostly corporate presidents, he asked them to choose any number from zero to nine. They had to make the choice 100 different times. When the executives had finished their part of the experiment, an IBM computer, which was programmed to operate at random, also selected 100 numbers. Each of the executives had one chance in ten of hitting the correct set of numbers; therefore, an average guesser would have been right 10% of the time. As it turned out, the men who had managed to double their corporate profits in the previous five years had an average score of 12.3% — substantially above the average.

Time magazine, January 11, 1971

32

Meanwhile, the executives whose companies had reported relatively low profit gains or outright deficits scored only 8.3% on the guessing test. In a second test, out of 25 other chief executives, 12 had doubled profits in the previous five years. Eleven of that group scored above 10% in the test. Of the 13 who had failed to double profits, seven scored below 10%.

On the other hand, a pattern may be undesirable, bringing into being the opposite results. Mostly, thanks to exposure to both beneficial and harmful conditioning, consciousness combines aspects of both into one highly individualized aggregate of a nature determined by earlier learning or experience. Against this cumulative mass, which becomes progressively more inert with age, isolated divergent conscious thought is ineffective. Only concerted internal and external effort can bring about a change of consciousness and of the resultant life pattern.

Consider the case of John, a highly intelligent young man, conditioned since early childhood by his parents' often repeated warning, "You will never amount to anything." Unless he has learned to disbelieve the word of his elders or is by nature a rebel, this pronouncement will become subconsciously established in him. After a promising start in college, induced primarily by his conscious effort to succeed and by his hope to prove his parents wrong, he seems capable of making the grade. But gradually the subconscious belief or fear that he will fail asserts itself. Because of its controlling role the subconscious will win. After his poor showing in school, John's conviction that he will not succeed in life increases.

Bravely, he tries his luck on a business career. His appearance, his qualifications, and his aspirations are superior. His ability to get along with others may win him the friendship of all associates. Nevertheless, his failure-consciousness could doom him to mediocrity, while other, seemingly less able employees, conditioned to a more positive belief about themselves, are promoted ahead of him. Enviously, John calls them lucky. Deep down inside he may accuse his supervisor of partiality. In fact, the supervisor himself as a rule cannot explain his preference for the other man. "I don't know," he might say, "but he has that certain something John is lacking." That certain something is a higher level of consciousness.

Turning to marriage, John could select a lovely bride, seemingly ideal for him. After a while, however, in spite of mutual conscious effort, discord may develop, followed by the inevitable divorce. After each setback John will mourn his tough luck. He might blame his professors, his boss, his wife for being against him. With righteous indignation, he may point out how hard he tried and how unfair the others were. "Poor John," his well-meaning friends may agree, "he certainly deserves better."

Causative Functions:

By properly understanding the causative function of consciousness, it is possible to trace John's pattern from his latest disaster through the preceding years of frustration to the first incident responsible for his inner belief in failure. Frequently, we carefully hide these embarrassing experiences from our conscious self. This does not mean that they are forgotten. Experiments by Dr. Wilder Penfield, director of the Montreal Neurological Institute*, have shown that by stimulating the temporal lobe cortex of any individual with a gentle electrical current *it is possible to achieve clear recall of incidents from the past,* down to the least word or detail. The cortex apparently contains a continuous strip of cinematographic film filled with our entire waking record from childhood onward. Each successive conscious experience is laid down in a relatively permanent pattern. This proves Einstein's contention that time has no independent existence apart from the order of events by which we measure it.

*Reported in "Some Observations on the Functional Organization of the Brain," donated to the Smithsonian Institution in 1956.

A skilled analyst does not have to resort to such complex techniques. From just a few significant incidents in a person's life, he is able to deduce the underlying pattern. For instance, a suitor is rebuffed by his sweetheart. He is also denied admission to the college of his choice. Later, a social organization turns down his application. In each case, the reasons given for the negative action may differ, but the cause is the same. The individual concerned has a deep-rooted belief that he is rejected by others or, stated differently, a fear of being rejected.

Counselors unfamiliar with these facts usually advise our friend to pick another girl, school, or club. In extreme cases, they may urge him to move to another city. Because they are concentrating on effects, their efforts cannot produce a lasting change. As we have seen already, our outer world is merely the visible counterpart of our inner world. *We carry our consciousness with us wherever we may go, producing the same results over and over again.*

Conditioning:

In a similar manner, Mark, a child forced to remain quiet and out of sight while others speak and occupy the domestic limelight, may become conditioned to this sort of treatment. The resulting subconscious pattern will have remarkable consequences. At school, at play, at social functions he would be shunted aside automatically from the mainstream of events. As Mark grows older, head-waiters may seat him at an obscure table next to the kitchen as a matter of course. At the office, he may be treated with indifference. And, accustomed to being on the sidelines, he will take his role for granted. It has become the norm for him. The very thought of being in the middle of things horrifies Mark because it goes against his grain — his subconscious expectation. We can now readily see why children with an opposite pattern can climb to the top wherever they are without effort. Once their mind has learned that they are important, it automatically creates the situations and opportunities necessary for their scholastic, social, professional success.

6. CHANGE OF CONSCIOUSNESS

Only when we change our consciousness can we expect the permanent replacement of an undesirable pattern. This change starts with giving the individual concerned an understanding of the reasons for his past experiences. Gradually, step by step, it is possible to remove his old beliefs.

Most of the beliefs controlling us are accepted by us at an early age. Although we have consciously long outgrown or discarded them in the light of adult understanding, the part of our subconscious containing this knowledge has remained at the age of its acquisition. In such cases, it may be necessary to go back to that age and make sense to the youngster in us from his level of understanding until he grows up to where we are. This external therapy will be especially effective if assisted by self-hypnosis or autosuggestion on the part of the individual, combined with a conscious effort to avoid a relapse into the old habits he desires to escape. We have shown students how to better their grades, efficiency, and attitudes by this unique means. The famous work of Emile Coue'* also should be mentioned here.

Purposeful action in accordance with the preferred pattern will accelerate the establishment of a new consciousness, particularly when reinforced with a positive speech pattern. Such words as "I cannot," "It is impossible," "I need," "I am tired," and "I always have trouble with . . . " act like negative suggestions on our consciousness, regardless of the connection or the degree of seriousness in which we may articulate them. They will help to produce future failures, difficulties, and states of exhaustion when and where we least expect them. For *our consciousness,* being ever operative, *determines our perform-ance or experience in all fields of activity.* The golfer who constantly gripes about his inability to break 80 may, without realizing it, also help ruin a business deal or his marriage. An engineer dwelling unduly on his tough luck in the stock market could very well contribute materially to the *failure of a major project* at his office. The housewife with the habit of thinking and talking

---

Self Mastery Through Conscious Autosuggestion, by Emile Coue'. New York: American Library Service, 1922.

about her fatigue after certain chores may wonder why she has trouble staying awake during an important social function.

During a guest appearance on the Mike Douglas Show, co-hostess Pearl Bailey told us (and the viewing audience) how, by constantly rehearsing "Tired," the song that made her a star, she wound up so exhausted that she was forced to concentrate on more beneficial topics.

In each case, the mind is loyally and impartially carrying out the orders given it in the form of thought, word, deed. And, unless counteracted by effort in the opposite direction, the mind will re-create the pattern established by a single impression-making idea or experience on an ever-increasing scale until it dominates us.

Results:

Even if we think or speak negatively about others, the results will be felt by us, since the subconscious is not concerned with the association of our words. Neither is it concerned with the person to whom they refer. It records them all with precise objectivity, thus assuring their permanent inclusion in our consciousness. The words, "He is no good," will be translated into, "I am no good," and backfire on the speaker in the future. As a matter of fact, *the only person we ever speak to is ourself.*

By applying these principles in a constructive and systematic manner, we have helped a considerable number of individuals to change from fear to confidence, from sickness to health, from failure to success after other professionals using conventional therapeutic or counseling methods had failed or termed the cases "hopeless."

One client, able to move about on crutches only, was instructed by us to tell her mother, whom she resented because of her professed helplessness, "You can do anything you want to do!" Within a few weeks, the client was able to walk normally again, although physicians had prepared her for further deterioration of her condition.

By the same principle, repeatedly uttered death wishes for oneself or others tend to come true, either for the speaker or his would-be victim, usually without conscious effort on his part.

In a recently published book, "Joe, You Could Have Made Us Proud," former baseball star Joe Pepitone reports that after one of many quarrels with his father, he shouted, "Mom, I wish he'd die. I really wish he'd die." His father, 39 years old, died of a heart attack the next night.

The tendency of successful people to live longer than others less fortunate is assumed by the Metropolitan Life Insurance Company, one of America's largest and most respected insurance companies, as a result of a 12-year follow-up study completed in 1968, to be due to physical fitness, intelligence and psychological stability. Principal credit, we assert, should go to a habit of winning and the basic inner direction (B.I.D.)* which as a rule is established by genetic, unconscious, subconscious and conscious factors, while functioning on a conscious as well as subconscious level.

Returning to John in our earlier example, we can now readily see how the countersuggestion, "You will succeed!" or, even better, "You are a success!" would work after diligent removal of the old mental habit. Each repetition would serve to penetrate his old failure-consciousness, assuring entirely new results in due course.

*as defined by us in *Victimology: An Effect of Consciousness, Interpersonal Dynamics and Human Physics*

New Patterns:

In the case of our young friend who has learned to shun the limelight, we would teach him that he can be — that he is — important. We would force him to insist on the choice seats in restaurants and theaters, to buy the best suits, and to become active socially, mingling freely with those he formerly considered superior to himself. By thus making him go from one extreme to another, the old consciousness will be broken and give way to a new pattern. For *the mind believes what it sees* (Mark is important, for example) *and then sees what it believes.* Later, a happy balance between the two extremes can and will be achieved.

Well known, in this connection, is the experience of couples apparently unable to have children who become parents in their own right after adopting one or more youngsters. Their unreasoning subconscious has accepted the fact that they now have a child or children. Once the mental rule of childlessness is broken, the appropriate body changes follow to ensure conception.

A child reared in poverty or injured in accidents or taught to expect hostility from others will be conditioned to expect this the rest of his life. Diligent, concentrated suggestion, combined with exposure to new environmental conditions, can bring about a complete change of consciousness, especially if our subject is young. Even the rather diffuse process of suggestion through routine educational means, television, books, or contact with people holding different beliefs may be helpful.

Pure State of Mind:

Of course, the reverse is applicable as well. Exposure to persons, teachings, or experiences of an undesirable nature can contaminate a relatively pure consciousness to the detriment of its owner. Every child, for example, is born with such a pure conscious state of mind, only to acquire from his parents, playmates, schooling the attitudinal awareness that determines the pattern of his life. Well-meaning missionaries, it is obvious, can quite innocently induce sickness among primitive tribes merely by making them conscious of conditions other than health.

The rapid spread of epidemics in the middle ages is plainly ascribable to factors related to consciousness. They were epidemics in the sense that the ailment spread like wildfire, but not necessarily because of any germ or virus. According to the British Medical Journal of February, 1970, they appear to have been the medical equivalents of the social "madness of the crowds," common a few centuries ago. We believe such phenomena can be explained in terms of mind. The same holds true for the rash of Western and crime movies on television, the rock-and-roll craze, the sportscar, van and other fads.

Children:

The imitative effect of consciousness is easy to observe, especially in children. Newborn babies want to walk early but current child-rearing practices block this response, according to Psychologist Philip R. Zelanzo of the Harvard University Department of Social Relations. He and his fellow researchers reported (on June 5, 1972) a "walking reflex" in infants that begins in the second week of life and continues until about the eighth week. If this instinct to move the feet were given an opportunity for expression, rather than allowed to disappear during this critical period, it could be maintained until independent walking begins, they believe. Earlier walking would result in possibly earlier learning as well.

This is evident from other developments. According to Francis A. J. Ianni of the U. S. Office of Education, several experimental projects were started to teach reading and writing to two- and three-year olds, fundamentals of algebra and economics to first graders, relativity and physics and the writing of music to second and third graders. In a speech to the Council of Chief State School

Officers in New York on November 16, 1964, Ianni deplored resistance to change by educators and parents. This resistance we ascribe more to subconscious than to conscious factors. As a result, the project was abandoned.

Mental rather than physiological factors are, we assert, responsible for another undeniable phenomenon. Puberty is steadily advancing in boys and girls. According to an English pediatrician*, it arrives about three-tenths of a year earlier each decade. At one time, the average age was 16. It is now 13. If the same rate is maintained, the average in 50 years will be close to 11. The appropriate learning about adult behavior, acquired by means of television, reports by peers and observation, comes first. The resultant desire to be "grown up" triggers off accelerations in body development.

The selective use of suggestion can have beneficial effects on a far-reaching scale. Harsh criticism, whether applied in schools, industry, or at home, is bound to induce a consciousness that will produce even more conditions requiring correction.

7.   BUSINESS USE

It is now readily understandable why the wording of letters, announcements, reports, and advertising matter is of critical importance. *One word or statement can make the difference between a desired or undesired result.* Going one step further, carefully evolved *suggestions can assure marked improvements in the performance of* pilots, students, executives, salesmen, workers, or *any person in any field of endeavor.* In this connection, it is quite feasible to raise the efficiency of skilled technicians far beyond the predictions based on carefully evolved Human Factor studies.

Chicago Daily News, "Sex Is Getting To Be Kid Stuff," June 9, 1969.

The use of appropriate language can assure the success of sales campaigns and other projects. This type of communication is based upon the writer's freedom from doubt, fear or hesitation. Therefore, it cannot help but evoke a favorable response by the addressee.

8.   BRAIN AND INTELLIGENCE

Contrary to popular belief, brain size is no indicator of intelligence. After Albert Einstein's death, anthropologists were surprised to find that the great man's brain weighed little more than 5.5 pounds. Brains of "average" people weighing as much as nine or more pounds have been encountered. We believe we have an explanation for this phenomenon. Original thinkers don't bother to acquire and store often useless knowledge or habit patterns. They draw directly upon the universal intelligence that is available to us all.

C.   GROUP CONSCIOUSNESS

1.   FAMILY

So far, we were concerned primarily with the consciousness of individuals. By extending our considerations to the group level, we can learn more about the important laws of mind.

The old saying, "Birds of a feather flock together," expresses a profound truth. The members of a family may differ in appearance, temperament, and interest. Inevitably, though, they have in common basic characteristics of consciousness. When this pattern is one of harmony and love, all is well. A predominant belief in, or fear of, discord makes quarrels and frustration inevitable. An underlying lack-consciousness will produce economic hardship. *The basic mind pattern of the group produces uniform effects on all members.*

As individual members of the family travel, move elsewhere, or form new associations, their consciousness undergoes an inevitable change. This may result in a sort of mutual estrangement. "Mary sure has changed since she went to college," a mother might say, or, "After Jim joined the Army, he just grew apart from us." Nobody can pinpoint the reason for these developments in terms of a physical cause, although we may blame specific individuals or circumstances. What really took place was that Mary and Jim acquired a new, or modified version of their former, consciousness. Sometimes, an individual with an unusually strong consciousness can raise or lower the level of belief of an entire family, thus assuring its continued togetherness. More frequent, however, is the case where the gulf between the two divergent forms of consciousness widens. This will lead to inevitable separation as the years go by.

Conversely, a person marrying into a family with a different consciousness cannot hope to achieve lasting harmony without considerable adjustment. As time passes, provided a desire to get along exists on both sides, some of his consciousness will be absorbed by others, while he may acquire theirs. *Like not only attracts but makes like. At the same time, it repels all that refuses to become alike.*

In the absence of other consciousness factors, a sick-conscious husband may attract a wife with a similar consciousness. Their children, as a rule, will display symptoms of a corresponding nature.

By the same process, alcoholics, card players, musicians manage to attract each other. Not uncommon is the case where two pickpockets try to victimize each other. A salesman without money, as a rule, will attract prospects in a similar financial predicament.

Supposedly objective public opinion pollsters tend to encounter persons who hold views similar or identical to their own. Unless the polling team reflects proportionately all viewpoints of the total population, its findings will not be accurate.

A man returning to his hometown after years of absence may find he has nothing in common any more even with his most intimate boyhood chums. His consciousness, and theirs, has changed so much that he is out of tune with them. To paraphrase author Thomas Wolfe, "You can't go home again!"

2. SPORTS

A team with a uniform will to win, i.e., a win-consciousness, is invincible. Let the team be joined by a new member who formerly was with a loss-conscious outfit. Because of the contagious nature of consciousness, he will become one with his new environment.

On the other hand, like a bad apple spoiling the batch, a player with a deep-rooted loss-consciousness can contaminate his more positive associates and cause them to lose game after game. Although the coaches may concentrate on improving the technical aspects of his game, they are wasting their time unless they succeed in changing his consciousness.

3. INDUSTRY

In industrial situations, the consciousness of the president is crucial. By the law of attraction, the members of the management team will have the same basic consciousness. Management, in turn, may attract employees with a consciousness identical to that of the whole.

Let us assume that Company A has a success-consciousness, while Company B is failure-conscious. Although both may hire managers and technicians with similar qualifications as far as education and experience are concerned, those joining A differ from the others in their inner beliefs about themselves and their future. Projects tackled by A as a rule will satisfy the customer, while B's efforts may be subject to criticism or failure.

Eventually, *as individuals change their consciousness, they drift apart from the general level of mind prevailing in their organization.* Water always seeks its own level. A man feeling himself worthy only of $10,000 a year may automatically reject or be rejected by others in a $20,000-a-year consciousness. Some employees may resign to associate with another company conforming to their state of mind. Asked for a conscious explanation of their action, they may point to a better salary or other physical factors without realizing that they were actually responding to invisible causes. Similarly, they may be terminated, not because of incompetence, but because they have a subconscious insecurity or inability-to-please pattern.

It is obvious, of course, that presidents and managers also change their consciousness with time. As a result, company policy and performance will not remain the same either. Some individuals, progressing faster consciousness-wise than the organization, may terminate to go to greener pastures. Others, not progressive enough, will remain behind to grumble about the implemented changes, eventually seeking more compatible affiliations elsewhere.

What should be noted is that *groups always are harmonious in that they conform to one central belief pattern.* This pattern is what each member, from the leader on down, has in common with the other. The harmony principle applies even where there is apparent discord. For the discord is an outward projection of the inner consciousness of all the members. The conversion of even one individual to a pattern of inner harmony and peace would destroy the homogenous nature of the whole and necessitate his parting company with the rest.

To illustrate the effect of consciousness further, take the case of two real estate companies. One spends thousands of dollars on newspaper advertising, the other seems to have buyers and sellers automatically flock to its doors. This requires only the occasional placement of a small ad, which always brings immediate results. The difference is not better salesmanship or listings but belief. The first firm is governed by the conviction that "moving" houses is difficult and expensive. The second firm has a consciousness of being in an "easy" business. It knows that its listings are in demand and its ads read.

A similar case in point is General Motors, a company with unquestioned success-mindedness. Every year, its president predicts unprecedented production and sales figures, knowing that they will be met with only slight deviations. This belief is the cause, while the resulting mechanical, promotional, administrative, and sales transactions are the effect.

4.   SUCCESS

A film called "The Habit of Winning," first shown to the Sales Executives' Club in New York City on May 19, 1972, features the business success stories of several men who played for the late Vince Lombardi, famed coach of the Green Bay Packers. Jerry Kramer made a big score on an apartment project in Oklahoma and is now in the cattle business in Idaho. Fuzzy Thurston and Max Magee own a growing chain of restaurants in Wisconsin. Willie Davis has a flourishing beer distributorship in Los Angeles. Paul Hornung is successful in real estate and other businesses in Kentucky and Florida.

Lombardi once said: "Running a football team is no different from running any other kind of organization — an army, a political party, a business. The problems are the same. The objective is to win." Under his leadership, the player acquired and perpetuated the appropriate state of mind.

The remarkable number of general officers (36% out of 164) emerging from West Point's class of 1915 ("The Class the Stars Fell On") — Eisenhower, Bradley, McNarney, Van Fleet, Stratemeyer were among its illustrious names — may also be explained in terms of mind rather than physical coincidence.

5. SAFETY

In a more tragic application of the basic principle, the National Safety Council used to forecast grim motor accident totals before each holiday weekend. Not only are these totals reached almost every time but exceeded on many occasions.

Our examples demonstrate the power of consciousness when combined with the power of suggestion. In each case, management is sure of itself. This attitude alone suffices to produce the desired result. However, the responsible individuals generally believe that publicity is necessary for success. This confidence in advertising, followed by suitable action, is a secondary factor in guaranteeing the ultimate result. The public, in turn, responds to the powerful suggestion with automatic precision, especially because of its trust in the issuing agency and an already existing predisposition to believe, based on past performance. Repetitive exposure to such a campaign exercises an almost hypnotic effect on suggestible individuals who, compelled by subconscious motivation, are mostly unaware that they are responding to the will of others.

The automobile company with the greater success-consciousness is able to outsell a competitor. In the case of a traffic campaign, the published warnings act as commands to be careless or to get killed. For the mind translates the words, "Be careful!" into, "You are careless." Because of the reproductive power of the mind, this amounts to, "Be more careless!" Of course, we must not overlook the effect on our consciousness of the additional suggestions we receive when viewing the products advertised, be they homes, new cars, crashes or mangled bodies.

Our desire to share our research and experience along these lines with responsible officials and the general public prompted us to call on the Automobile Club of Southern California in February 1957. We also contacted the National Safety Council. Instead of publicizing the 400 to 500 expected fatalities per holiday weekend, we suggested that emphasis be put on the 100,000,000 or so people who would reach home safely. As is customary with original information that contradicts contemporary knowledge, we were greeted with polite skepticism.

Later we were visited by Joseph P. Havenner, the executive vice president of the Auto Club, to whom we presented our findings in detail. Nothing was done, however. The accuracy of our contentions was confirmed later in an article entitled, "Scare Tactics Impede Traffic Safety: Researcher," by Dr. James R. Adams, Safety Research and Education Project, Columbia University, published in the March 1962 issue of *Traffic Digest and Review* of the Traffic Institute, Northwestern University.

Jaws:

After the release of the movie, "Jaws," a general fear of sharks kept many swimmers on shore. Author Peter Benchley, who wrote the smash hit, narrowly missed being ripped apart by a vicious seven-foot shark. It happened early in July, 1975, off the Bahama Islands, while millions were lining up to see the movie version of his book. On July 16, 1975, 14-year-old Beverly White sustained severe cuts on her arm when bitten while swimming less than 200 feet off New Smyrna Beach in Florida. On July 23, 1975, a 14- to 18-foot shark seized Robert Rebstock, 23, a skin-diving U.C. Santa Barbara student, who was dragged to safety by his companions. ("All of a sudden," said Tom Hesseldenz, 22, "Rob just rose out of the water. He shouted. It was amazingly like the movie . . . ," apparently referring to "Jaws.") Four days later, on July 27, a 12-foot shark seized surfer Gary Grace, 21, then spat him out in an attack 300 yards off Maroochydore Beach in Sydney, Australia.

A large shark is reported to have attacked and devoured Bobby Ray Slack, an American-born commercial abalone fisherman, near Hobart, Australia, on July 21, 1975. There were other reports of shark attacks throughout the world in the summer of 1975.

A less frightful illustration of the effect of consciousness on events pertains to the 15,000 shark jaws Ralph Ferguson had stored in his warehouse in Wilmington, California. For years, they gathered dust. Suddenly, according to the Los Angeles Herald-Examiner, dated August 12, 1975, when the movie "Jaws" was released, the phone started ringing off the hook. Amusement parks and retail stores ordered thousands of the jaws. Individual buyers from across the country wanted to take the jaws home as souvenirs. One retailer bought several crates of jaws and came back the next day hollering, "How many more can I get?"

Similar mental factors may well have been responsible for the outbreak of fires in a Century City (Los Angeles) high-rise building shortly after the release of "The Towering Inferno." The same movie also came too close to truth for comfort on July 11, 1975, when a group of film and television agents were trapped, along with hundreds of other occupants, for almost two hours on the 18th floor of a burning skyscraper in midtown Manhattan.

Mental contagion of this sort is also involved when prison riots, strikes, kidnappings and other events occur almost simultaneously in various parts of the nation or the globe.

Even government upheavals belong in this category. President Franz Jonas of Austria died of cancer on April 23, 1974. Willy Brandt resigned as Chancellor of West Germany on May 6, 1974, after a top member of his staff was convicted as a spy. Several weeks later, on August 9, 1974, President Richard M. Nixon left his office because of the Watergate scandal. In Japan, Premier Kakuei Tanaka resigned on November 26, 1974, after his popularity had dropped to 18.8% and an unusual exposé of his interlocking personal wealth and political power.

D. UNIVERSAL CONSCIOUSNESS

1. MIND AS A CONTINUUM

Brain emanations or waves know no limitations of time or space. Experiments in telepathy all over the world have proved that thought is unaffected by the thickest wall or the greatest distance. To test the theory that we all are miniature broadcasting and receiving stations, highly perceptive individuals were sent complex mental messages over great distances. They recorded and understood them with amazing clarity. Specially conditioned or natural mediums can react to suggestions transmitted by thought over great distances as if they had been given orally at close hand.

Since 1950, Dr. W. H. C. Tenhaeff of the University of Utrecht, Holland, and his team of telepathists* have by telepathy located missing children, objects,

---

*Reported in *This Week Magazine (Holland's Incredible Mind Readers*, by Jack Harrison Pollack) on February 19, 1961.

criminals, pets. Some of these gifted people, according to this reputable, world-famed scientist, can "see" the past and future, as well as the present. They can describe events taking place miles away, unseen by anyone. They can "know" intimately a person they have never met simply by holding something belonging to him. They help solve cases of smuggling and espionage for their government.

In 1959, Peter Hurkos of Holland* visited the National League spring training camps, soaking up "electricity" from the players and their dirty uniforms in the laundry baskets. As a result, he predicted that the Los Angeles Dodgers, who finished seventh in 1958, would win the pennant. He also foresaw the final standings of the other seven teams. He was dead right. Besides, in 1957, he tabbed the round and winner when Ray Robinson regained his middleweight boxing title by knocking out Gene Fullmer in the fifth.

Until a few years ago, ESP — extrasensory perception — occupied the scientific doghouse, although the Soviet Union had for some time displayed an avid interest in what its scientists have now come to call "biological radio." Its application to outer space has been the subject of intense speculation and experimentation.

Soviet ESP Experiment:

Describing a unique Soviet ESP experiment, using a mother rabbit and her newborn litter, Dr. Pavel Naumov is quoted as saying: "As you know, there is no known way for a submerged submarine to communicate with anyone on land. Radio doesn't work. Scientists placed the baby rabbits aboard the submarine. They kept the mother rabbit in a laboratory on shore where they implanted electrodes deep in her brain. When the sub was deep below the surface of the ocean, assistants killed the young rabbits one by one. The mother rabbit obviously didn't know what was happening. Even if she could have understood the test, she had no way of knowing at what moment her

*Reported in *This Week Magazine (Extra! The "Radar Brain" Picks Pennant Winners!* by Leslie Lieber) on April 26, 1959.

children died. Yet, at each synchronized instant of death, her brain reacted. There was communication, and our instruments clearly registered these moments of ESP.*"

ESP as a reality in everyday life is easy to observe. Even nonbelievers in psychic phenomena often think of an individual just a moment before encountering him or hearing from him. Also not uncommon is the case of a creditor receiving payment for the amount due him as soon as he decides to make a firm demand upon the debtor. In each instance, there occurred extrasensory or, actually, suprasensory communication.

Until recently, physical scientists in the United States and elsewhere have tended to ridicule parapsychology as a doctrine of the occult. According to a recent article in the Los Angeles Times, rocket engineers are now talking to theologians about ESP and clairvoyance, biochemists and physicians are studying faith healers, and conservative research institutions are experimenting with mind over matter.

PSI:

Since 1973, an unprecedented $200,000 in federal grants has gone into psi (for psychic phenomena) research. The National Aeronautics and Space Administration funded a Stanford Research Institute study on ESP. The Defense Department's Advance Research Projects Agency paid for a Rand Corporation translation of all Soviet literature on paranormal phenomena. The National Institute of Mental Health funded a study on dream research at the Maimonides Medical Center in New York and the U.S. Navy is entering the field. The CIA will neither confirm nor deny its rumored activity in the area of parapsychology, but several scientists claim they were approached by the agency, and that

---

*Psychic Discoveries Behind the Iron Curtain, by Sheila Otrander and Lynn Schroeder, Englewood Cliffs, N.J.: Prentice-Hall, Inc., 1970.

it is indeed involved. One California scientist, according to the *L.A. Times*, professes to know of a study involving the "sensory shielding" of the U.S. President to prevent anyone from reading his mind. The American Psychological Association, with 30 different divisions, would not even include parapsychology among them until a few years ago. Among the most determined exponents of research into paranormal behavior are laser physicists Russel Targ and Harold Puthoff of the Stanford Research Institute. In 1974, they conducted highly controlled experiments on Israeli psychic Uri Geller and others.

By correctly guessing 12 out of 12 times which of 10 double-sealed cans had a steel ball and which of 15 cans held water, Geller beat trillion-to-one odds.

By correctly calling the face-up number in a dice in a sealed box eight out of eight times, Geller beat million-to-one odds.

He also was able to create a "significant magnetic field" — presumably through psychic energy — and affect the weight, both plus and minus, of a one-gram object, employing what may or may not be psychokinesis.

In another experiment, Geller was placed in a room shielded visually, acoustically and electrically from drawings he was asked to duplicate. He did so 10 out of 10 times, a chance of probability of better than one in a million.

Former Astronaut Edgar Mitchell, the sixth man to set foot on the moon, founded the Institute of Noetic (perceptive) Sciences, headquartered in Palo Alto, California. It largely encouraged and funded the Geller experiments. The Institute is also establishing five professional research chairs. One, the chair in physical sciences, has been named in honor of Werner von Braun who, after being in rocketry and physics all of his life, now says that noetic sciences hold the only hope for the salvation of civilization.

We have found that the majority of signals involved in interpersonal communication emanate from a level higher than the conscious and subconscious. Therefore, we have learned to speak of SSP (suprasensory perception). Too numerous even for partial listing here are the carefully recorded and verified cases of ordinary individuals learning positively, without visible or audible means, of certain events, as a loved one's death, in another part of the world.

Millie Coutant's vision of a trailer and a blue pickup truck with Carolina license plates served as the essential clue in locating Joanne Tomchik's two young daughters. "If it wasn't for her," Mrs. Tomchik said, "I'd still be looking for my children." Lisa, 5, and Amy, 3, weren't returned to their home in Burnt Hills, New York, by their father after a visiting day in April, 1972. On February 22, 1974, Tomchik and the girls were found in Wilson County, North Carolina, in a trailer, the blue truck nearby.

A few years ago, Mrs. Leticia Shindo, 47, of Scottsdale, Arizona, had a premonition that Mr. Grover, an ill friend 60 miles away, needed help. At this very moment, Grover, an ailing 58-year-old bachelor, was being held prisoner at gunpoint in his isolated little home by two multiple murderers who had escaped 24 hours earlier from the Arizona State Prison in Florence, 7½ miles southwest. With the aid of her son George, 18, and George's best friend, Dennis Roeper, 17, she coolly executed a plan which resulted in her friend's liberation.

The reaction of dogs and other creatures to the human consciousness is well known. Many instances are on record where animals traveled over remarkable distances to find their owners. In late 1963, Mrs. Giovanna Ashley of Sacramento, California, gave her five-year-old German shepherd-collie to a friend about 30 miles to the north. Three days later he returned, thoroughly tired out. She tried again a year later. She drove the animal to her stepdaughter's house 60 miles away in Yuba City. She figured he couldn't walk home again. But, two days later, he was at her front door.

For years we have observed and taught that animals reflect the consciousness of their owners or other humans. The applicable principle is demonstrated by the following case.

Mental Transmittal:

A worried mother consulted us because her eight-year-old daughter had left notes around the house in which she expressed her intent to leave. The school psychiatrist was puzzled. This mother and her husband loved their little girl. She, in turn, loved her parents and could not explain her strong determination to run away from home. We traced the cause to the mother. As a child, she had wanted to leave her parents because she felt unloved. (No doubt, she had responded to the parental consciousness.) Although she had repressed her impulses, she married — in accordance with the law of consciousness — a man whose behavior restimulated them. Again she exercised repression without, of course, realizing that her daughter would act as a reflector and expressor of her hidden desires. We helped this woman to adjust to her mate (who also had an escape consciousness, though in application to his job) and marriage. This diminished her and the child's get-away urges. These were transmitted, however, to the family dog who disappeared three times. When the responsible consciousness was changed permanently, the pet never left again.

On August 18, 1964, a team of psychiatrists at Hahnemann Hospital in Philadelphia, Pennsylvania, released a report confirming the accuracy of our teachings along these lines.

Animals also respond to certain stimuli in a manner resembling that of humans. A UPI report, dated June 5, 1973, tells the story well.

"Chessington Zoo has found a new way of increasing its chimpanzee population — showing the chimps sex films. Zoo officials said they recently showed their chimpanzees a British Broadcasting Corp. television documentary presenting chimpanzees kissing and cuddling.

"Most of the Chessington chimps loved it and copied every move," said zoo spokesman Andy Bowen. He said one six-year-old female chimp named Cressida was 'turned on and overcome with passion.'

"We hope to hear the patter of tiny chimpanzee feet here soon, and all thanks to the film," Bowen said. "We tried it on three cages of ape houses," he said. "The orangutans were only interested in the projector. (Our comment: Further proof of the reflection principle in action!) The gorillas became aggressive but Cressida was just overcome with passion."

Cressida particularly swooned over the chimp male star of the film — "the equivalent of Rudolf Valentino for her," Bowen said.

Brain Waves:

Another known phenomenon is that two or more people in widely separated places can make the same invention at the same time, quite independent of each other. They are merely tuned in to the same brain wave frequency. Also, uneducated people often pick great ideas out of thin air or discover profound truths that eluded the so-called "brains" whose consciousness was conditioned along orthodox lines. After all, who taught the Fultons, the Edisons, the Fords, the Wrights? These men never went beyond grade school.

Observations have shown that the pain experienced by one twin as a result of an unscheduled operation or accident is often perceived at the same time by his counterpart who is thousands of miles away and totally unaware of the cause of his sensation.

All this makes possible the conclusion that *the mind is an infinite continuum* encompassing our entire world, including all mankind, all animals, and all objects. In this gigantic field of electroprotonic wave motion, each creature has a rate of vibration or individuality all its own. Going one step further, the same goes for every mood, activity, experience. A house or car will retain the vibrations of its owner. If these are of a low nature, they can depress a visitor or new occupant. If high, they can stimulate him.

2.   MIND DYNAMICS

Brain waves, unless changed, *are beamed by each human individual to a suitable receiving consciousness to cause the emergence of a corresponding result.* Dr. Ainslie Meares, an Australian medical hypnotist*, discovered that people in a trance pick up subconscious messages easily and may learn something the doctor does not want them to know. The thought, "This man will never get better," even by an attendant, for example, will have a harmful effect on the patient.

This sort of transmittance, we contend, is taking place at all times, also between unhypnotized persons. The fear by a mother that her son will have an accident, by a husband that his wife will criticize his late arrival home, by a wife that her husband will cheat on her, by an employee that his boss will fire him, by a defendant that the jury will vote against him, by a salesman that his prospect will not buy can thus induce the appropriate response. Conversely, positive attitudes or beliefs will cause a favorable reaction by the other person.

*Reported in the November 1959 issue of *The Practitioner*, London, England.

Everything that happens is influenced not only by the consciousness of the interested parties but by that of apparent outsiders as well. A murderer with a conscious or subconscious desire to kill will be attracted to his victim because of the victim's fear of being killed and because others, including his family, neighbors, the police, are crime-conscious. Of ten grocers in a section of town, one may have a wife with a particular fear of holdups. This could result in his repeated victimization in spite of guns, other counter-measures, and his wife's absence from the store. Her negative expectation will be and must be fulfilled until replaced by a greater confidence in protective remedies.

News releases and motion pictures about these incidents only heighten the already prevalent consciousness of evil and produce further crimes. The juvenile delinquency situation illustrates this principle graphically. Because of the general expectation of incidents along these lines, adolescents with only a latent tendency for trouble making are compelled by forces they cannot understand to act in a manner they may later bitterly regret or be unable to explain. Everybody who knows them will say, "Bill always was such a good fellow!" or, "I would have never thought that Mike could do such a thing!" And Bill or Mike will assure his parents or police, "I just don't know what came over me!"

3. CYCLE-COMPLETION PRINCIPLE

Expectation Fulfillment:

The subconscious mind always produces a completed cycle or whole. It will go to any length to fulfill an expectation. Its work is not done until an accident-conscious person has had an accident himself or until an accident involving him indirectly has happened to a close relative or friend. The same holds true for success-, obstacle- or any other type of consciousness.

In our files is the case of a man who became a human "torch" while spraying his backyard with a fuel to burn off weeds. While his clothes were afire, the unfortunate victim began running around, the lit torch still in his hand, crying, "I knew this would happen — I knew it!"

Miami Police Sergeant Charles Crocker had trouble holding his weight down to 200 pounds, so he went on a crash diet six weeks prior to starting a vacation in 1969. By dieting, he felt he would not have to watch his weight so closely while vacationing. After drinking some orange juice, he complained to a fellow officer: "This diet is killing me." Moments later, the 35-year-old policeman toppled off a canteen stool, dead of an apparent heart attack.

True confidence attracts to man what he wants. Fear brings him what he does not want. This is apparent from the following account, published in the Santa Monica Outlook of August 13, 1975:

"A man who lived in terror of crocodiles was eaten by one 15 feet long with three legs and no tail in far north Queensland, a coroner's inquest was told today.

"The inquest into the death of Peter Reimers, 35, was told he was so scared of crocodiles he never would wade in water more than a few inches deep.

"Witnesses told Coroner B. J. Blades they believed the crocodile was aware of Reimers' habits and stalked him for days before it took him at the end of a hunting trip on April 26.

"Reimers was sitting in shallow water cooling off at the time.

"Two work friends from the giant Weipa bauxite deposit and police constable A. C. Bone found his severed legs at two separate points along Mission Creek near the waterhole.

"Marks on the legs indicated a crocodile attack and they threw explosives into the waterhole, they said. The crocodile, which surfaced and disappeared, was later dragged from the water dead.

"Reimers' body was found inside in eight pieces.

"Police told the coroner they believed the crocodile had lost its tail and one leg in a fight with another crocodile. Fully intact, it would have measured 20 feet."

Mitla:

Along more cheerful lines, the citizens of Mitla (population 6,000) in the Sierra Madre Mountains of Southern Mexico "don't expect crime because they don't know what it is," according to their mayor, Eliseo Diaz, as quoted by Dudley Freeman, New York reporter for the London Sunday Express (September 2, 1973). Mitla is without parallel in the world. For the past 100 years it has not had a single crime. The doors of the town jail are always open. Children are born, raised and buried without ever seeing a patrolling policeman. They are trained not to fight but to remain law-abiding. They let off steam by throwing a twig at the offending child's foot. But without hitting the foot. This they recognize as the severest form of criticism, and the children never go beyond that. The jail is used only by those who have drunk too much mescal at the bar and do not feel like lurching all the way home. They sleep it off in jail.

Anthropologist Dr. John Paddock of Stanford University made a study of Mitla's people. He says: "These folks are totally peaceful and their respect for the rights of their neighbors is absolute. They work hard, play hard, but remain united. It is fascinating how they and their forebears have never committed a crime. Clearly they have stumbled upon something which the rest of the world could use. Other towns in the region have murders, rapes, and robberies, while Mitla is the only crime-free town in the world, as far as is known."

Regional police commissioner Gonzalez Cortez said: "We have never stationed a policeman there. It would be a waste of manpower."

Marital Selection:

According to Vance Packard*, husbands with an inner desire for domination are in the habit of selecting mates with domineering proclivities, wives afraid to speak up have unusually outspoken mates, and jealous spouses have counterparts who seem to give them reason for their jealousy.

Going one step further, these people do not select each other. They are brought together by the controlling mental factors to make a whole, although physical factors appear to be responsible. Each in every word and action, is reflecting the other's subconscious. In reality, *every person we know or meet mirrors a part of our own self,* in all he says or does.

We should mention here that, because the subconscious reproduces what one has learned about people in early life, one's mate often resembles or is identical to the parent of the opposite sex in attitude, behavior and/or appearance. Accordingly, he or she may be fearful, cold, obese or given to drinking too much. People also tend to model themselves, by conscious or unconscious imitation, after the parent of the same sex. In case they resented this parent, they may pattern themselves in the opposite direction. For example, they will be especially neat, strict, or generous, in contrast to this parent.

An emotional projection test developed at the University of Colorado Medical Center indicates that we see our emotions — and ourselves — in others. Persons taking the test are asked to identify emotions expressed in a series of thirty

*Reported in *Look* magazine (*Why We Marry As We Do)* on June 10, 1958.

portraits. The subjects inevitably reveal their basic personality traits by their interpretation of the emotions expressed in the portraits. Indeed, "it takes one to know one."

We have done much research along these lines. Satisfied people usually see other people as enjoying the same consciousness. Critical persons will dislike those who find fault with others. They do not realize, as a rule, that they are looking into the infallible mirror of life. Men fearful of financial ruin often belittle others for being afraid of social embarrassment or strangers. These persons share the same consciousness, although its manifestation may differ through what we call a transformation effect. When those who formerly had an undesirable consciousness, such as that of perpetual problems, acquire a more confident outlook on life, they will become especially conscious of their former attitude in friends and strangers they encounter. They see their past state of mind reflected by others.

Case History:

The following case from our practice will illustrate this point further. A husband complained that his wife would scream at him whenever he was a few minutes late for dinner. The woman was unable to explain her behavior which was entirely against her nature. Although she made conscious attempts to control herself, her outbursts increased in vehemence. The husband, in comparison, seemed incapable of avoiding his late arrivals.

Careful diagnosis showed that as a youngster he learned to associate being late for dinner with being screamed at by his mother. In fact, he never knew what to expect from her. The conditioned reflex created in this manner resulted in a subconscious pattern which transformed a perfectly sweet and loving woman into a veritable shrew. Because the subconscious repeats what it has learned, his home as an adult was equally unpleasant as his childhood home. Each scene merely intensified his fear of coming home. This, in turn, created a pattern of being late over which he eventually lost control.

The wife, in contrast, had a hidden fear of losing her husband and of hurting people unjustly, the result of a consciousness implanted by well-meaning but ignorant parents.

An important point is that, since our subconscious expectations originated in association with a parent, brother, teacher, or other person close to us, the one behaving in like fashion toward us inevitably is a person important to us — our mate, boss, friend.

Now we can see why early criticism-mindedness can produce a lifelong pattern of criticism. The location and the people nagging and reprimanding us may change, but the unpleasant reproaches will continue, in spite of sincere efforts to please on the victim's part.

In a similar way, teachers attract students, doctors attract patients, employers attract employees, sellers attract buyers, contractors attract subcontractors, the police attract wrongdoers, and vice versa. We can also understand the relationship between persecutor and persecutee, majority and minority groups, and the strong and the weak.

Negative Consciousness:

In the event of unpleasant experiences, the victim with the negative consciousness may swear on a stack of Bibles that he or she did not think along the undesired lines at the time. There is no doubt that this is so, as far as *conscious* thought is concerned. Consciousness, though, comprises the entirety of our pattern. And *thought,* as a definite form of energy, *is neither created nor destroyed.* It remains effective even years after its conception by us to produce the necessary result when circumstances are suitable for effecting the "thought-about" event.

A woman secretly afraid that she is not good enough for her husband may succeed in hiding this from her conscious self. However, her seemingly nonexisting expectancy of marital disaster has already made inevitable the appearance of the other woman. The unhappy wife, naturally, will blame her mate and the *femme fatale.* A sympathetic judge, ignorant of the psychological causation, will agree. But even if the illicit affair were to stop, soon another woman would enter the picture. And so on *ad infinitum,* until the wife changes her consciousness.

Once the cycle or whole has been completed, the stage is set for the start of a new cycle on an even larger scale as a result of the intensification of our mind grooves from the impact of the preceding experience. *This is also the best time for implanting a more desirable pattern* by means of the already-recommended steps.

Example:

We now will present an example of how people unknown to each other are drawn together by their subconscious because of separate reasons having in common one crucial factor. All the facts, except the names, are true.

Margie, a cute four-year-old, while dashing to an ice cream parlor ahead of Mrs. Black, her mother, stepped on a heel of backless shoes worn for the first time by Miss White, a glamorous model, causing Miss White to fall and break her nose. To all appearances, the child was to blame. The model sued Mrs. Black for a large sum of money. Our investigation revealed the following facts which resulted in an out-of-court settlement.

Miss White, we found, had been taught by her mother since early childhood that her face was her fortune. She feared harm to her valuable features. About six months prior to the accident, when buying the already mentioned shoes in a Long Beach, California, store, she told the clerk in jest, "First time I wear these, I'll probably fall flat on my face and break my nose." In this manner, she unwittingly decreed how her latent and deep-seated expectation of facial injury would be fulfilled.

Let us consider now the consciousness factors pertaining to Mrs. Black. She was 13 and on the threshold of womanhood, as indicated by her first menstrual period, a most delicate time for any young lady. She and a girlfriend were walking down the main street of a little Arizona mining town, past the union hall where a large number of men were gathered as was their custom. Lo and behold, at that moment the elastic of her panties broke. Gracefully she stepped out of them. This incident would have gone unnoticed, had not Susie, her four-year-old sister, entered the scene. Certain that she was doing her big sister a great favor, she picked up the soiled garment, waved it happily after the horrified girl, and shouted, "You dropped your panties!" Mrs. Black would have preferred death to the amused laughs of dozens of grown men.

Consciously she had long forgotten this incident, but her subconscious retained its learning and growing expectation of embarrassment in public from little angels like Susie. Margie, until the age of four, was a joy to take out. Then, seemingly by coincidence, she began to do things embarrassing to her mother who felt compelled to spank her. The little girl had become conscious of spankings whenever she and her mother went out together. Because on the accident day she had been exceptionally good, Mrs. Black wanted to reward her with an ice cream cone.

Miss White, on the other hand, had driven twenty miles to get a specific kind of ice cream which could be obtained only at the ice cream parlor near the Black home. She parked her car in the only space available, smack in front of that home. Little did she know that at that very moment Mrs. Black was opening the door to launch a bubbly, vivacious guided missile named Margie in the direction of Miss White to fulfill their mutual expectations. Margie, with apparent deliberation, proceeded to step on the heel of Miss White's shoe as if ordered.

The following points deserve notice. Fear was the consciousness factor all three persons had in common. Miss White had a fear of losing her beauty and livelihood. Mrs. Black was controlled by a fear of embarrassment or loss of pride and dignity in public, but the association of this fear was transferred from her sister to her daughter. Margie, in turn, was conditioned into a fear of public spankings. Each fear, it must be pointed out, was unnatural or learned.

If permitted to continue in Miss White's case, for example, her subconscious, due to its habit of ever enlarging the effects of a predominant belief, might produce a situation in which her face would be marred to the point where she lost her livelihood forever, i.e., through a fatal accident.

Margie's subconscious association of physical pain with being in public, unless changed, would create progressively more serious instances of body hurt as she matured. Here are some examples of how her consciousness might express itself. As a teenager, she may be clumsy at school games and fall during a basketball game. Later, a boyfriend could slap her without reason in front of others or her loving husband, quite unintentionally, may slam a car door on her hand.

Also, the time periods involved here clearly illustrate that the subconscious knows no time.

When we explained to Miss White how her own consciousness contributed to the accident, she dropped her lawsuit against Mrs. Black and agreed to settle for nominal damages. After understanding all the pertinent factors, Mrs. Black and

Margie were able to resume the happy mother-daughter relationship that had existed before Margie became four.

4. BEHAVIOR CONTROL

That it is almost impossible to resist the compelling effect of consciousness has been demonstrated by our preceding examples. Often the results of this inevitable surrender to the hidden expectation of others can have far-reaching consequences for the lives of entire families or larger groups.

According to a common assumption, for instance, overweight people are clumsy. This belief merely tends to reinforce an already existing propensity. A notable exception to the rule was one of our clients, an agile calisthenics enthusiast. When alone and in the presence of his admirers, he could perform incredible feats. One day, while exercising near the swimming pool of a resort hotel, however, he failed miserably to come up to his usual standards. Those watching him, unfamiliar with his ability, simply could not believe that a man of his proportions was capable of such dexterity. He fell victim to their collective expectation. Later, when shown the reason, he tried again and succeeded.

The same principle governs the often seemingly inconsistent behavior of children. They may be loud and uncontrollable in the presence of one parent or both parents. While with relatives and friends, ignorant of this undesirable conduct, they can be veritable angels. The reverse may also be true. Youngsters at their best with parents may be literally hellions while with strangers. Responsible for this undesirable duality are the adults' general and specific concepts about minors.

A husband, considered cold, indifferent, and thoughtless by his wife, her mother, and best friend, changed for the better in a relatively short time when we instructed the wife to describe him to others as having the characteristics she desired. Not only was the belief of her mother and best friend changed in this manner, but the wife's own consciousness in time accepted as true her frequent telephonic and personal accounts of her husband's supposedly new behavior pattern. As a result, he actually did change, without ever knowing why.

One of our clients and students, an alert and dynamic insurance executive, usually was wide awake while attending our classes. When his wife was present, however, he usually fell asleep a few minutes after the lecture had started. Upon our request, the woman stayed away from class on three specific occasions. At those times he never got sleepy. We found this man to be, without his or her awareness, under the control of his wife's subconsciously established learning. As a child, she had become painfully aware of her mother's criticism of her father who fell asleep every time they went to a concert, family affair or function involving other people. Quite against her conscious will, she was now playing the same role as her outraged mother with regard to her spouse. In her subconscious, she had identified him with her father. We showed her the dynamics involved here and furnished her adequate proof that her husband often did not doze in public, especially when she was absent. As a result, her consciousness was modified gradually. At last, her husband could and did remain wide awake in her presence.

5.   OTHER APPLICATIONS

A company selling the public on its superiority can create such a demand for its products that it will gain leadership in its field by virtue of the powerful consciousness factors involved. Its merchandise may have been mediocre at the start, but the decisive effect of public confidence will unavoidably tend to bring about the necessary improvements. For the majority belief will govern and be rewarded, positively or negatively. The unconscious association in the mind of people of quality with a certain name or trademark after repeated exposure to comprehensive advertising campaigns cannot help but create an expectation beneficial for all concerned. On the other hand, adverse publicity can be equally detrimental. *The more people we can convince that something is so, the more certain we will be of the outcome.* Looking at a tragic example, Secretary of State Dulles's quick death after disclosure of his critical condition may be attributed not only to his own consciousness and that of his doctors, but to the expectation of a nation.

In refreshing contrast is the case of screen actor John Wayne. In perfect accord with our previously published recommendations, it was not revealed until his complete recovery, late in 1964, that he had an operation for lung cancer. In this manner, the public's expectation was utilized to the actor's advantage.

In the practice of voodoo, there are many well-documented cases of a perfectly healthy person lying down and dying after being informed of his bewitchment by the tribe and of his imminent death on a specific date.

In contrast, an athletic team, thanks to a clever publicity campaign, can win the confidence of millions, who may never attend the ballpark, to assure its triumph over technically superior opponents. Now we can explain why forecasts of inflation, disease incidence, unemployment, or accident rates usually are correct.

On a nationwide scale, a widespread poverty-consciousness can impede governmental attempts to achieve prosperity. The expectation of economic reverses by a large segment of the population can cause stockmarket drops and depressions.

6.   INTERNATIONAL IMPLICATIONS

Consciousness naturally plays a major role in international relations as well. For, as stated at the outset, these principles apply individually, collectively, and universally.

Even the present political division of the world, of Germany and Berlin, of Ireland, of Europe, of Korea, of China, into two separate factions is merely a universal manifestation of the split (see Chapters B and D, Part II) prevailing in the individual mind on earth. This duality is characterized by such alternatives as "I want to, but . . . ", "you should" or "you shouldn't," and "he (they) should" or "he (they) shouldn't."

From our extensive research it is evident that a nation's headman may find his words and actions misunderstood to such an extent that he is reacting, in response to the underlying subconscious mass expectation, with anger, indignation or — in an extreme case — a declaration of war he himself would not be able to justify upon sober reflection when removed from the compelling mind influence. For *a country's consciousness of being opposed by another nation or group of nations must bring into being the corresponding hostility.*

Here again the principle of association can be observed in action. As an illustration, the sinking of the U.S.S. Maine precipitated the Spanish-American War. This seemed to have the effect of a nationwide conditioned reflex. For when the S.S. Lusitania was torpedoed by German submarines, the United States eventually entered World War I. Later on, the destruction of the U.S.S. Arizona, West Virginia, and other warships by Japanese bombers precipitated U.S. participation in the Second World War.

Nations with a predominant peace-and-harmony consciousness like Sweden or Switzerland will have a better chance than countries with a history of repeated wars to remain aloof from international trouble. Citizens of these countries, it should be noted, also enjoy a high degree of personal security, as far as employment, health care, and other freedoms are concerned.

The true measure of a country's war-mindedness is not profession of peaceful intent by its government and citizens but the number of its involvements in and concern with armed conflict. Here again the repetitive and accelerative effect of belief is visible. The periods of peace between major wars have become shorter and shorter. The wars themselves have produced increasingly more casualties and destruction.

Thanks to the universal emphasis on undesirable conditions, we live in a world conscious of war, disease, poverty, hunger, and other tragedies. The already demonstrated power of mind to manifest and reproduce the object on which our attention or consciousness is focused makes inevitable the prediction of a bleak future for the world. *Determined and intelligent countersuggestion on a universal scale is necessary* to stem this growing trend. Although it is clearly impossible at this time to change the mind of the earth's entire population, our willingness to make a start with ourselves can have beneficial effects beyond our expectation.

To resist and rise above the prevailing tide of negation requires individual discernment of what constitutes a desirable attitude and course of action. Uncompromising refusal is required to surrender to the hypnotic effect of mass hysteria, accompanied by consistent behavior along the lines that seem preferable.

E.   CONSCIOUSNESS AND MECHANICAL PERFORMANCE

1.   NATURE OF MATTER

From the preceding discussion it is clear that *consciousness affects not only* people and animals but *objects* as well. This deserves special emphasis.

Consciousness and matter, as was shown in Chapter B, actually are the same due to their identical electrophysical nature. As a result, the conclusion is logical that *matter*, being crystallized consciousness, *has* or, actually, is *intelligence*.

Many findings tend to confirm this. Damaged portions of the brain do not die but instead are reorganized and "rewired," a University of California (Irvine) team of researchers reported in 1972. James L. McGaugh, chairman of UCI's psychology department, said the findings represent "a phenomenal discovery with almost science-fiction implications for the treatment of brain disorders." Previously, cells from one embryonic organ were completely reshuffled by Drs. Paul A. Weiss and A. Cecil Taylor of the Rockefeller Institute in New York*, yet they retained their amazing ability to organize themselves and remake the organ from which they came, whether it was a miniature kidney or liver. This demonstrates that cells under proper condition can reconstitute themselves into a particular organ without outside direction. They contain their own information about their particular job in life.

Plants also have intelligence. Nobel Prize winner Luther Burbank expressed his love in word and feeling to roses, assuring them that they need not fear outside harm. After three generations, they had shed their thorns.

**Drs. Mark A. Stahmann and J. C. Walker of the University of Wisconsin told the American Chemical Society that plants such as bananas, tomatoes, and peas can suffer "strokes" and "heart attacks" caused by clots in their veins just as humans suffer from clots in their blood vessels. Researcher Sterling B. Hendericks and his co-workers of the U.S. Department of Agriculture at Bethesda, Maryland, shaded a group of little pine trees during part of the day with opaque cloth. In accordance with the phenomenon whereby plants hasten their own growth when they feel winter approaching, the sprouts bloomed months early. Also a large corporation's scientists, attempting to grow plants upside down to simulate the non-gravitational conditions of outer space, found that the plants became confused and suffered "nervous breakdowns" or "complete frustration."

---

*Reported in the Proceedings of the National Academy of Sciences on Oct. 15, 1960.

**Reported in *This Week Magazine (Revolution Rocks The Plant Kingdom,* by Leslie Lieber) on June 26, 1960.

Dr. Rhine's famous experiments at the Parapsychology Laboratory of Duke University* have shown that *the mind can produce a physical effect upon an object.* Concentration on specific results when tossing coins or dice caused attainment of the expectation in a number of cases exceeding significantly the laws of chance. Convincing proof was furnished of human ability to perceive external physical objects. Distance, size, and number of objects did not affect the results. This is merely a scientific confirmation of the "mind-over-matter" theory.

Even more dramatic is proof furnished by the aforementioned Uri Geller, a young man of piercing gaze. According to the serious columns of London's *Sunday Times* as well as numerous other publications and TV programs, he has shown that he can make spoons curl up by his touch and broken watches tick again.

This principle can even be demonstrated under ordinary conditions. While shaving with a new electric razor in a public men's room, a client of ours was told by a stranger that he had purchased a similar model whose head fell off the third time he used it. As soon as the stranger left, the client had the identical experience.

2.   PERSONALITY AND OBJECTS

That consciousness affects matter is further illustrated by the fact that houses, rooms, items of clothing eventually assume individualized natures conforming to the personality of their owners.

Cars come off the assembly line identical in appearance. After a while, they differ appreciably. While the initial product inevitably represents the maker's consciousness, it soon begins to reflect also the consciousness, the true personality indicator, of its owner. That is why navy ships of the same class in

* *The Reach of the Mind*, by J. B. Rhine, New York: William Sloane Associates, Inc., 1947, pp. 156 and 157.

due course acquire a personality of their own, indicative of the captain's and the crew's state of mind and feelings. The identical dress worn with pride by its happy owner will look drab and wear out sooner on a woman with a defeatist attitude.

A woman we know constantly praises her articles of possession. They remain beautiful and retain their new look for a long time.

Every new owner's consciousness quite naturally modifies the original product in accordance with his individual state of mind.

We frequently found that defects in the plumbing of certain homes reflected stomach or other internal disorders of the owners. A leak in the radiator of a new high-quality automobile baffled the dealer and his mechanics. Our investigation disclosed that the vehicle reflected its new owner. She was suffering from a kidney disorder which had deprived her temporarily of control over her urine.

By way of elaboration on a phenomenon previously discussed, an owner's belief in a certain make of car can result in smooth, satisfactory service. A person critical or skeptical of the same trademark may attract a "lemon" or cause a car to become troublesome although it previously pleased another with a desirable attitude.

A secretary with an inner rebellion against her boss or job can, without knowing it, be responsible for frequent breakdowns of an actually flawless electric typewriter.

According to her own report on a Steve Allen television program, in May, 1964, actress Olivia de Havilland found herself trapped three times successively in a private elevator which had never malfunctioned before. Significantly, she had just completed the motion picture, "Lady in a Cage," in which the breakdown of a similar conveyance served as the basis of the drama.

Another illustration showing the effect of consciousness on matter is the different longevity of houses in Europe and the United States. The peoples on the other side of the Atlantic are accustomed to homes hundreds of years old, considering them fit for further occupancy. As a result, the buildings retain structural stability. In this country, on the other hand, a house after only a few decades is regarded as ready for condemnation. Because it naturally shows the corresponding wear, the structure has to be torn down.

The consciousness of supposedly inanimate objects also affects people. One of our clients suffered suicidal depressions. When we could not find a cause in her, we investigated her environment. We found that she had recently moved to a certain apartment whose previous two successive occupants had, totally unbeknown to her, taken their lives. We suggested that she move to a new place that was free of the adverse consciousness factors. She quickly regained her former cheerfulness. Couples in the habit of quarreling constantly over finances and other matters began to enjoy harmony and freedom from monetary pressure after taking up residence, as advised by us, in homes formerly occupied by prosperous and loving families.

Places, too, have a consciousness all their own. Some of recent history's bloodiest campaigns were fought on fields which had served as battlegrounds for many centuries. By the same process, unbeknown to ministers and congregations, their churches often stand on sites where former civilizations had built houses of worship. Bars or dancehalls usually do not succeed on such locations. Conversely, churches built on ground formerly used for other, more frivolous or commercial purposes, often fail to thrive. The consciousness in control dictates their removal to more suitable places. Many promising business organizations, unaware of the applicable dynamics, lease premises where former tenants or owners had failed. Eventually, they do likewise. Relocation to quarters with a more favorable consciousness could and usually does result in improvements in the firm's fortunes.

On August 27, 1964, a hit-and-run motorist jumped the curb and ploughed into a line of four sapling magnolia trees planted in the parking area in front of a Brentwood, California home. "This is the third time this has happened in the past few months," commented the gardener. "I sure wish those drivers would watch it."

Donna Lunn Lew, 19, of Palm Springs, was killed on February 27, 1970, the second fatal shooting to take place in the same Cathedral City apartment.

In 1969, three vehicles in less than six months plunged into the yard of a Los Alamitos, California home from the San Gabriel River Freeway.

3.   APPLICATION TO AVIATION AND OUTER SPACE

Probably nothing demonstrates the role played by the mind in human affairs better than the history of flying. Primitive man considered aerial transportation as a dream practicable only for the birds. The Greek legend of Daedalus and Icarus acted as an early conditioner on the human race. As a result, generation upon generation of young people, at least during their impressionable years, speculated on the possibility of flight. Gradually, the general level of expectation was raised. When Leonardo da Vinci drew his pilot models of airplane designs, the universal debate on the feasibility of flight started in earnest. Nostradamus's famed predictions merely added fuel to the fire. Before too long, the first balloons rose from the ground.

Flying had graduated from the consciousness of a few daring individuals to that of the entire race. The first flight of the Wright brothers was a logical result. However, general unbelief, especially in the reliability of the first airplane engine models, was common. Combined with the understandable fear of the pilots, their next of kin, and the ground crews, this widespread consciousness of uncertainty caused many crashes. Every plane taking off had to overcome, in addition to structural and mechanical difficulties, the adverse mental attitude of a major portion of the world's population. Only step by step did the airplane gain the universal repute as a safe mode of transportation it enjoys today, thanks in no small measure to the conditioning effect of ingenious and constant advertising by the airlines.

Another excellent example illustrating the same principle pertains to the famed Bermuda Triangle. In this mysterious region, more than 100 ships and aircraft, including 1,000 people, have vanished without leaving a trace of evidence. Several skeptics attempted to explain these accidents in terms of science and not parapsychology. This, we suggest, is not significant. What matters is that they occurred in the first place.

We can now see why Buck Rogers and other science-fiction stories play a vital role in the advancement of mankind in general and of space flight in particular.

Setting the stage for man's first manned moonflight was not just President John F. Kennedy's May, 1961 decision that a U.S. team would set foot on the moon before the end of the decade. Ample conceptual preparation preceded it.

The first trip to the earth's satellite was described in *True History* by Syrian theoretician Lucian of Samosata, in 150 A.D., followed 14 centuries later by Bishop Francis Goodwin's *Man in the Moone* (1638). *L'Autre Monde; ou, Les Estata et Empires de la Lune* by Cyrano de Bergerac, in 1657, came next. The eminent Johannes Kepler, in 1638, completed a scientific vision of the trip, entitled *Somnium.* Professor George Tucker of the University of Virginia, writing under the assumed name of J. Atterly, came out with *A Voyage to the Moon* in 1827. This also was the title of a book, published in 1864, by English clergyman Chrysostom Trueman. Edgar Allan Poe wrote *The Unparalleled Adventure of a Hans Pfaal* in 1835. Jules Verne's famous *From the Earth to the*

Moon followed in 1865. Later he also wrote *Round the Moon* and *Trip to the Moon*. H. G. Wells completed *The First Men on the Moon* in 1901. Fritz Lang directed *Frau Im Mond* (Girl on the Moon), his motion picture about moonflight in 1929. More recently, in 1950, film producer George Pal directed the much-acclaimed "Destination Moon," written by famed science fiction writer Robert Heinlein.

We obtain a good idea of the time lag, called lead time by engineers, required between conceptualization and realization of an idea when we note that 18 centuries elapsed from 150 A.D. to July 19, 1969, the day Neil Armstrong and Buzz Aldrin took "a giant step for mankind" to make a dream come true.

Noteworthy from our viewpoint is the fact that Armstrong was the eldest of three children (subconsciously he learned early to lead two others). He took his first plane ride at the age of six, earned a pilot's license before he drove a car, won praise for several outstanding combat missions in Korea and tested the X-15 rocket plane.

Young Armstrong's heroes were the Wright brothers, Orville and Wilbur, the mechanical wizards out of a bicycle repair shop in nearby Dayton who made the first controlled flight of an aircraft. Armstrong's mother said: "He read everything about them. He thought they were just the greatest of men."

Aldrin was known as a typical team man, in sports and at West Point (where he finished number 3 in his class). According to our deduction, as the second child of his parents (a sister, Fay Ann, was 1½ years older; another sister was 3½ years younger) he was predestined to be number two on the moon. His father, Colonel Edwin Eugene Aldrin, Sr., U.S. Army, retired, served at intervals as military aide to General Billy Mitchell, whom young Buzz Aldrin met as a boy of five. (Genetically, we believe, he was pre-programmed to serve Armstrong, the Number One man!)

Michael Collins, who deplored the fact that he had to remain aboard the command module while his teammates cavorted on the moon surface, was also preconditioned for his role. Born in Rome when his father was a military attache' at the U.S. Embassy, Collins was an "Army brat" who also lived in relative isolation at a succession of Army posts during his childhood. Typical is his early complaint that he had to look on from the outside and couldn't play with the native youngsters in Rome, Puerto Rico and elsewhere. He traveled more than the other astronauts in his childhood. Consequently, it came as no surprise to us that Michael was chosen to travel around the moon, without ever setting foot on it.

F. CONCLUSIONS

We believe the preceding discussion shows that man, despite considerable technological advances, is still in the Dark Ages when it comes to understanding his own natural resources. In terms of the individual, these are his thoughts, feelings, words and actions. Formal education, at least in its present state, apparently does not suffice. This is illustrated by most of the preceding examples, especially those involving physicians and other men of learning.

Ignorance of the dynamics presented here is, unfortunately, still widespread. The common practice of complaining, in jest, about bleeding ulcers, headaches, aching backs and visual difficulties may stem from a desire for sympathy or getting out of an unpleasant job. Invariably, our research has shown, it is translated into painful reality. In the case of tennis star Jimmy Connors, it may have cost him the 1975 Wimbledon Championship. He has become famous almost as much for his on-court antics as for his two-fisted powerplay.

Well known is Connors' habit of repeatedly pratfalling while clutching his chest and screaming, "Oh, my heart, my heart!"* On one of these occasions, Connors had a sudden onset of chest pains and thought he had suffered a real

*TIME, April 28, 1975.

attack. A check-up at Marina Mercy Hospital in Marina del Rey, California proved negative. Earlier in 1975, Connors had pulled out of other tournaments with vague ills. This makes understandable the charge by some tennis fans that he was faking. However, after his stunning upset by Arthur Ashe at Wimbledon, Dr. Andreas Cracchiolo, a UCLA orthopedic surgeon, on July 17, 1975, said Connors was indeed suffering from a painful injury in his lower right leg when he lost to Ashe. Because the tennis star did not mention his condition, his doctor called him a tough kid. Perhaps ignorant would be a more appropriate word!

Word Patterns of Presidents:

One may expect such naivete from a brash 22-year-old athlete but hardly from well-educated, supposedly brilliant politicians. Yet, Richard M. Nixon and John F. Kennedy were victimized, according to our deductions, more by their word patterns than by their lack of know-how or effort.

"I am going to campaign up and down America," said Nixon in his famous Checkers speech on September 23, 1952, "until we drive the crooks and Communists and those that defend them out of Washington." As if to prove that an individual's subconscious can determine not only his destiny but that of a nation and the world, Nixon eventually won the presidency and became involved in conduct which, as a trained lawyer, he himself could not help but call crooked. By the same token, in earlier years, he had in effect endorsed Sen. Joseph P. McCarthy's position that dealing with the Soviet Union and what was then called Red China was tantamount to being a Communist. These rules were recorded in his subconscious.

It should be noted that Nixon made his historic trip to Mainland China from February 23 to 28, 1972. On June 17, 1972, five men with electronic surveillance devices were seized at Democratic National Headquarters in

Washington's Watergate Building. These two events combined to serve as triggers for the subsequent political spectacle that culminated in Nixon's resignation. He and almost all the men he had picked were, true to the words he spoke almost 22 years earlier, "driven" from Washington. It should also be noted that Vice President Spiro T. Agnew resigned on October 10, 1973, after pleading "no contest" to one count of income tax evasion.

Nixon and many of his defenders complained about the relentless fury of those intent upon exposing his conduct. He merely was getting a dose of his own medicine. California Representatives Jerry Voorhis and Helen Gahagan Douglas, who once were targets of Nixon's wrath, can testify to this, as can many others. He was felled by the same tactics that had catapulted him to the top.

Nixon's guilt feelings were perfectly offset by criticism from the courts, the Congress, the media and the public. As soon as President Ford gave him an unconditional pardon, this balance was destroyed and he almost died from phlebitis.

John F. Kennedy:

Without excusing Lee Harvey Oswald or any other assassins who may have acted together with him or apart from him, we contend John F. Kennedy removed himself from the President's office, his family, and his body by similar means. On October 26, 1963, in a nationwide telecast, he had demanded ". . . changes in policy if not personnel" in the Diem government, which he also deprived of vital C.I.A. funds. It may be quite true that he had not actually ordered the assassination of the Diem brothers five days later, and, as has been rumored, that of Cuban Premier Fidel Castro. But the mental factors involved here were sufficient to bring about the events at Dallas on November 22, 1963. As we have shown in our paper on Victimology,* there were others.

---

*Victimology: An Effect of Consciousness, Interpersonal Dynamics and Human Physics, presented at the First International Symposium on Victimology in Jerusalem, Israel, on September 4, 1973; later published in the International Journal of Criminology and Penology, December, 1974, and Lexington Books, Lexington, Massachusetts, 1974.

That Richard Nixon was in Dallas, on business, on the tragic day was, to us, more than a coincidence. Mentally, he was quite attuned to the dashing President who had defeated him at the polls more than three years earlier. Both men were ambitious, tenacious and acknowledged leaders of their respective parties. But each took in his own way his promises lightly. Nixon, his oath of office; Kennedy, his marriage vow — as has by now become well known.

In this respect, he followed in the errant footsteps of his dapper father. By the law of action and reaction, as translated by us into its Human Physics equivalent, this contributed to whatever happened to each: resignation in disgrace for Nixon, assassination for JFK and ignominious recall from his ambassadorship at the Court of St. James, as well as a stroke, for the father.

The subconscious, we suggest, does not care whether a word is broken with regard to one aspect of life or another. Men may try to make a difference by calling one an inexcusable perfidy and the other a masculine prerogative. But the impartial, ever-operative internal computer doesn't. It has precedence even over a papal dispensation.

It is great to have power, great to have wealth. But greater than both, in the long run, are honor, integrity and righteousness.

On May 27, 1959, in reply to a letter from a friend of ours* reminding him that no President elected in a year ending in zero had survived his stay in the White House, the future President wrote that he had never reflected on the matter, that it was "indeed, thought-provoking," and "should anyone take this phenomenon to heart . . . anyone, that is, who aspires to change his address to 1600 Pennsylvania Avenue . . . most probably the landlord would be left from 1960 to 1964 with a 'For Rent' sign hanging on the gatehouse door."

Shortly after the 1960 election, his own father said, "Jack is the fellow who will give his life to his country." In his inaugural address, JFK said that "we

*Harry A. Squires of Granada Hills, California

shall pay any price . . . " On the same occasion, he referred to the time as one of " . . . maximum danger."

Kennedy and Lincoln:

Many other factors contributed to what happened later. Chief among them is young John Kennedy's yearning to be another Abraham Lincoln. Accordingly, his subconscious recorded the following sequence of events: (1) Election to President, (2) Involvement in Civil Rights, (3) Assassination. As soon as Kennedy had achieved his first objective, the second became an automatic reality, on a basis modified by contemporary circumstances. Eventually, he didn't have to look for an assassin. By the mental forces at work, he became a magnet that drew Oswald — or, for that matter, anyone in a complementary state of mind — to himself.

Other principals on the scene also helped. Under the direction of what we have decided to call the total prevailing mind, each contributed to the formation of the environmental womb required to give birth to a perfect baby — an assassination (see Fig. 1). Among them was Jackie Kennedy (later Onassis), who, at 17, was present when her beloved horse, Donny, had to be shot, and who had berated herself for her absence, in 1957, when her beloved father died a lonely death in a Manhattan hospital.

Lyndon B. Johnson:

There also was Lyndon B. Johnson, who had a pattern of gaining the office he sought only after the incumbent's death. Johnson had become a U.S. congressman in 1937 after Texas Representative Buchanan's death and a U.S. senator in 1948 after Senator "Pappy" O'Daniel's passing.

FIGURE 1

PRINCIPAL CONSCIOUSNESS FACTORS INVOLVED IN KENNEDY ASSASSINATIONS

John F. Kennedy

1. Loss to Joe, Jr.
2. Sickness
3. PT 109 Sunk
4. Death of Joe, Jr.
5. Operations '54/55
6. Bay of Pigs
7. Joe, Sr.'s stroke
8. Patrick's death
9. Saigon Coup
10. Assassination Pantomime

Jacqueline Kennedy

1. Parent's divorce
2. "Donny" shot
3. Rejection
4. Jack's near-death
5. Miscarriage
6. Still-born child
7. Father's death
8. Patrick's death

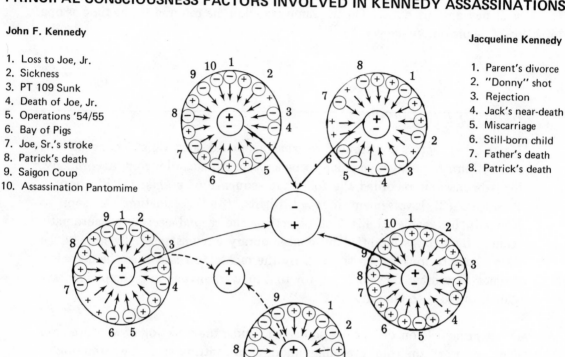

Lee H. Oswald

1. Early Insecurity
2. Orphan's Home
3. Mother's second marriage
4. Youth House
5. Marine discharge
6. USSR & Return
7. Suicide Attempt
8. "Fair Play" for Cuba
9. Failure to kill Gen. Walker

© C. K. & J. M. Teutsch 1964, 1973, 1975

Jack Ruby

1. Parents separate
2. Foster Homes
3. Union Co-Founder
4. Army Air Corps
5. Move to Dallas
6. Club Ownership
7. Union Expelled
8. Incidents
9. JFK assassination

Lyndon B. Johnson

1. U. S. Senator - forecast
2. Ex-Gov. Neff Introduction
3. "I'll be President" (at 21)
4. Election to House after Rep. Buchanan's death
5. Loss to O'Daniel
6. Victory over Gov. Stevenson
7. Sen. Majority Leader
8. Ike's prediction
9. Heart attack
10. Loss to JFK, VP nomination

We trust it can now be seen why we regard every individual as the upper stage of a multi-stage missile launched into a specific orbit which has generally been established prenatally — before birth. What we have come to call the individual's B.I.D. (Basic Inner Direction) usually reinforces, but sometimes modifies, the basic trajectory.

At any rate, a thorough knowledge of life patterns by JFK and his advisers would have precluded the selection of the tall Texan. In fact, JFK himself should not have been permitted to run, we assert, without submission to a program of the type we have developed.

Therefore, we feel justified in asking that aspirants for high office, in addition to being examined physically, should be examined for their proneness to assassination. This could well prevent future national or worldwide disasters of this sort.

Laws:

The facts presented by us indicate that human behavior and experience in general derive not from chance factors but from the operation of laws that are as precise and generally applicable as those governing the universe.

Not directly opposed to our views but likely to solve only part of the problem is the view of authorities, such as Dr. Jack R. Ewalt, superintendent of the Massachusetts Mental Health Center, Bullard Professor of Psychiatry at Harvard, and president in 1964 of the American Psychiatric Association. At the APA's convention in Los Angeles he described as an unsolved challenge the question of what to do about people who are not "mentally" ill but who have little control over their aggressive urges.

"In a social sense they are more deviant than many an ambulatory schizophrenic," he said. This problem, according to him, was highlighted by the attack on President Kennedy. He also mentioned the tendency of people who cannot control their aggressions competently to associate themselves with extreme causes of a patriotic or revolutionary nature or both.

If such persons require study and special treatment, we assert, so do those who are potential victims. Human beings do not function independently of each other. Although therapy would undoubtedly benefit the would-be aggressor, it could not prevent other, so far peaceful, individuals from hurting or killing a fearful, harm-conscious or guilt-ridden person in accordance with his unspoken demand or unconscious expectation.

Murderers like Oswald usually do not appear to be potential assassins or potentially dangerous. In the presence of an examiner in a peaceful state of mind, they will tend to reflect his feelings. But they become dangerous when mentally or emotionally aroused by the overt or hidden hostility, fear, guilt, or death wish of a potential victim. A dog will bite only one who is afraid, not one who loves it. If animals respond to true human feelings, though covert, so, we maintain, do humans.

Proneness to Assassination:

These observations apply, of course, not just to the case of John F. Kennedy but to that of President Gerald Ford as well. Security precautions by the Secret Service no doubt will be strengthened because of the two recent attempts to kill the Chief Executive in Sacramento and San Francisco. But, in the long run, these may be ineffective. The victimizer or assassin is drawn, we assert, to his victim by the same irresistible force which holds the electron in orbit around the proton in the atom. Therefore, to prevent future national tragedies, a method should be found to examine Presidents not just for their physical health but for their proneness toward assassination. As far as we know, our TIM is the only available methodology capable of performing this crucial task in a single session.

The recent attacks on the life of President Ford are, to us, not surprising. He and his wife have adopted a permissive posture. They have given implied consent to conduct departing from the norm rooted in basic morality and the Bible. By giving a full pardon to Richard Nixon, the President in effect said that violators of the law should go unpunished, thereby inviting lawlessness. (The subconscious is not inconsistent. It will not discriminate between implied consent given to a President and an average citizen.) A house will fall on the one who weakens its foundation.

Unconscious Impulses:

On this same point, we testified before a judge and jury in Ventura County Superior Court in Oxnard, California, on February 20 and 21, 1971, that the potential victim's unconscious impulses elicited, at least in part, a law-abiding businessman's alleged conspiracy to do bodily harm to his ex-wife's attorney. Our explanations impressed the jury so much that they found the defendant innocent of all charges. Several jurors told us later they had confirmed the truth of our remarks in their own lives.

The defendant's attorney, as well as the many other attorneys among our clientele, feel that our methodology is one of the most effective tools for preventing miscarriages of justice.

But we believe our expertise extends further, and that we could, given the opportunity, show government on the local, state and national level how to eliminate energy crises as well as budget deficits. We can explain why, as many studies indicate, the poor pay more, and not just because of the greed of businessmen.

We can, as we did on June 26, 1967, help alter the trend of developments. On that day we were invited to the White House by Jim Jones of Lyndon Johnson's staff. During our discussion, we made a few suggestions. We pointed to some vital passages in the original version of this book. Next day, the President addressed the national convention of the Junior Chamber of Commerce in Baltimore. He said it was time to emphasize the "things that are right" rather than "what's wrong with America." The large audience, according to the Washington Post of June 28, 1967, repeatedly interrupted him with thundering applause. "He must have gotten hold of your book," some of our students told us. But since there obviously was no reinforcement, Johnson eventually returned to the very inner defeatism that resulted in his decision not to run again in 1968.

It is said that he had asked some physicians and statisticians how long he had to live. They predicted that he would not live beyond his 65th birthday. They proved to be right — primarily, we contend, because of Johnson's confidence in their verdict. Our TIM, we confidently assert, would have enabled us to extend his lifespan, as we did for several individuals whose family and medical history seemed to make inevitable their earlier demise.

As we demonstrated for the S.A.M.* group at the Washington State Penitentiary, in late 1974, it is possible to cut the recidivism rate of prisoners substantially. Several of these men had been treated by conventional techniques without success for many years. Just a one-hour session with us gave them sufficient insight and direction to preclude their reversion to their previous patterns. "If only you'd have talked to me before I did what I did," many said. "Why don't they have someone like you around all the time?" others asked. Most of these prisoners wanted to know why their state government or the federal government did not care to make this relatively inexpensive approach to crime prevention available on a larger scale. Their written pleas to Olympia and Washington remain unheeded, so far at least.

*Social Adjustment for Minorities

Our successes with individuals and groups also prove that we can substantially reduce traffic and industrial accidents. Typical of the attitude still prevailing in many high places is the comment of the National Safety Council official with whom we offered to share our expertise. "Do you wish to put me out of my job?" he asked.

One of the most vexing problems confronting the nation is, according to government officials from the President on down, the skyrocketing cost of medical care. The same holds true for the cost of hospital construction and maintenance and other factors. We are convinced that we can make a major contribution here. For proof, we point to some of the cases already listed in this volume. "Why don't the doctors at the National Institute of Health know what you do?" asked the Hodgkins' disease victim, whom we already mentioned, upon her totally unexpected recovery after more than three years of futile operations and other treatments. So did many other fortunate ones.

Losers into Winners:

We have begun to understand the solution to another major human problem: turning losers into winners.

One example was a gloomy encyclopedia salesman who it seemed just didn't make the grade. He was low man on his company's totem pole. Not long after we helped him to understand himself better, he became Number One in the country. Specializing in conventions, he established unprecedented sales and earning records.

Another example is that of a 27-year-old Chicano midget who was on state aid for the blind. He faithfully followed our advice. Paying his own way step by hard step, he stopped being dependent upon the state and is today the prosperous engineering coordinator for one of the nation's largest engineering firms. He also is happily married and the proud foster father of twins entrusted to him and his wife's care by the state.

We also have converted a number of individuals addicted to heroin and other drugs to useful citizenship in record time by means of mere discussion in accordance with TIM.

The key point is: we have taught people how to prosper, get jobs and be healthy, in spite of great odds or economic difficulties.

On the international scale, we can attribute many developments to the dynamics we have been describing. Mental factors, rather than political or military irresponsibility, underlie often puzzling developments. Some were involved when the once isolationist United States (the House of Representatives voted to extend the draft 203-202 in 1941, a few months before Pearl Harbor) became as militant (especially later in Vietnam) as had been the enemies once denounced as warmongers. Proof again that man often becomes what he loves or hates.

We have also found that the principle which governs the relationship between victimizer and victim for individuals can also apply on the collective scale.

In our paper on Human Physics we showed that the victimizer and the victim did not interact by accident, contrary to general belief, but were inseparable components of a functional unit existing in the same unified field.

The dynamics we discovered have their basis not in psychology but in physics as formulated by Newton, Einstein and others and as translated by us into Human Physics. As a result, for example, the fanatical hatred of the Palestinian and other Arabs for the Israelis can conceivably be viewed as partially emanating from the unconscious brain activity of the latter group. Either they or their ancestors learned to be victimized in Europe, and these experiences may well be responsible for their repetition on a modified basis at a new time and in a new place. The same principle is also responsible, we feel, for the situation in other trouble spots, such as Northern Ireland.

The deplorable *status quo* could be rapidly improved, we maintain, by the adoption on the collective scale of successful reprogramming techniques developed by us for individuals and their families.

When we presented our paper on this subject in 1973 at the First International Symposium on Victimology in Israel, our section head, Professor W. H. Nagel, an eminent Dutch criminologist, announced that we had either devised the most ingenious way for pulling his leg or found the answer to an age-old problem. After a private consultation with us, he conceded that the latter alternative was more likely.

We can point the way for the prevention of tragic occurrences by showing:

* Why brilliantly versatile actress Vivien Leigh, at 53, for example, died after a long siege of tuberculosis. She had played the consumptive Anna in Broadway's *Ivanov* for two years.

* Why actress Brigitte Bardot, who in the film "The Truth" slashed her wrists, later tried it in real life.

* Why actress Sharon Tate, who had died in the first "Valley of the Dolls" and whose husband, Roman Polanski, had made such macabre movies as "Knife in the Water," "Repulsion," and "Cul-de-Sac," together with four others became the victim of mass murder on August 9, 1969.

* Why Margaret Phillips, 25, a University of Michigan coed, who police said had been doing research into the slaying of six other young women, died in Ann Arbor on July 6, 1969.

We can also show the dynamics underlying the mass murder of eight nurses in Chicago by Richard Speck on July 14, 1966.

On the hilarious side, we can show the non-physical reasons for the emergence of a six-foot boa constrictor in the apartment of two Lawndale, California women.

Impact of Media:

The impact of the media, as we have shown again and again, on the singular and collective consciousness is undeniable. We do not favor censorship. But television authorities, as well as writers, producers and directors, should, we feel, be made aware of the important effect of their work, not only upon actors but upon the entire public. Many so-called experts claim that no proof exists to demonstrate the connection between events depicted on the little screen and actual life. We disagree. Our files are replete with cases that prove our point.

One of the best examples is the case of Evelyn Renee Wagler, 24, who was fatally burned when six youths forced her to douse herself with gasoline and then set her afire in Boston on October 4, 1973. The murder occurred only two nights after "Fuzz," a movie depicting similar attacks, was shown on nationwide television. "It's about time," said Police Commissioner DiGrazia, "that the public demanded an end to violence such as this in our movies and on television."

Recent developments show that the voices of DiGrazia and others are beginning to be heard.

The producer of the children's TV shows Sesame Street and the Electric Company claimed, on August 1, 1975, television is a "no-child land" because programming is still determined by the marketplace. "The real needs of the children simply do not count," said Joan Ganz Cooney, president of Children's Television workshop. She and two other experts rejected claims by questioners that violence and sex on television don't harm children.

Calling for a return to the attitude of nonviolence, Richard Allen, executive director of the Center for Social Research, on January 10, 1974, said, "We face the prospect of a society growing more lawless, more violent, more callous — more apt to turn fictionalized mayhem into real-life horror. It is a much more dreadful prospect than anything acted out in the appropriately titled 'Planet of the Apes.'"

Undoubtedly television has many desirable effects. Among them we may consider the case of Dwight Stones, U.S. and world high-jump champion. He was three when he watched Valery Brumel of the Soviet Union clear the bar at 7'5". "I'll do even better," he told his astonished parents, "when I grow up." He did.

Effect on Sports Events:

"Live" television has other so-far-unsuspected effects. *The National Star*, dated July 20, 1974, reported our finding, also mentioned by Tom Snyder on NBC Sports, that the mental radar of television viewers (and radio listeners) affects the outcome of sports events. The television or radio commentator's words to the effect that an athlete or team seem to be tired or not likely to make "it" tend to bombard the one or ones performing with inaudible commands to win or lose. The electrical activity involved here equals an invisible tug-o-war. It has the effect of millions of people in the stadium, shouting "Win!" or "Lose!"

The same dynamics can also influence the performance of actors, politicians, and announcers. In certain cases, therefore, delayed telecasts may well be advisable.

The favored Milwaukee Bucs did not win the 1974 professional basketball championship. The reason was, we suggest, that the team lacked the mental support of Milwaukee area fans during the final game because of a television blackout. This cancelled out the homecourt advantage. The Boston Celtics, on the other hand, had their fans rooting for them on television.

Nursery Rhymes:

For years, we have familiarized educators (some of them principals, vice principals and master teachers among our clientele), publishers and others with another important result of our research. Nursery rhymes in almost every nation tend to condition helpless youngsters toward fear, sickness, accident, and death. Jack and Jill, Little Red Riding Hood and others are cases in point. So is the folklore of most countries. Particularly in Germany, the young, at least until recently, were taught songs that prepared them to give their lives for the fatherland. To make sure that they did, statesmen, politicians, generals, industrialists and voters were impelled to act in a mostly unconscious conspiracy. Each group, of course, justified its actions in terms that seemed perfectly plausible but were actually mere rationalizations.

It is obviously not easy to make instant improvements in all these areas. We shall take a brief look at ways our know-how may be used to benefit the individual.

Self Concept:

One of the most important factors in determining human behavior and performance, something we pointed out orally more than 20 years ago and in writing five years later, is the *self* concept. It is established in several ways. One involves the manner in which parents and others relate to a youngster in thought, feeling and word. Another is the name by which he is called. Studies have shown that certain names have a downright undesirable implication not only in a child's own mind but in that of others.

Writing in the September, 1970 issue of *Science Journal*, Dr. Joseph Mallory Wober, Bristol University psychologist, reported that most girls at three schools thought Elizabeths and Rachels were likeable, attractive and intelligent. A similar American study found the name "Engbert" to be particularly unpopular.

In these instances, as in all surveys, we suggest that the personal bias of the interviewer cannot be ignored. He tends to elicit from the interviewees the appropriate response. But on one fact there was general agreement: People tend to grow into the personalities associated with their names.

A splendid example is Los Angeles Superior Court Judge Nancy Watson whose attorney father called her "Judge" from the time she was four years old.

Upon our advice, the parents of a clumsy little boy, who always suffered bruises from needless falls and other accidents, renamed him "Lucky." The improvement was remarkable. While still in kindergarten, he won a trip to Hawaii for the entire family on a game show.

Some parents name the first-born male "Junior" or "II" or even "III." Unwittingly, these parents set the stage for the perpetuation or reinforcement of some undesirable hangups or experiences. Invariably, we have found, individuals in this category benefited greatly from name changes.

Changes in last names can also be important in eliminating undesirable associations.

I. Q. Tests:

Along these same lines, the use of I.Q. or other tests to measure intelligence, personality or aptitude can have a deplorable effect on an individual's self concept. One of our chief objections to the I.Q. is its emphasis on verbal ability merely because the test's designer viewed that as the chief criterion for intelligence.

This very concept contradicts an important fact. *Everyone has specific and unique talents, in addition to being a genius of sorts in his or her own way.*

That is why such talents as color and space perception, memorizing numbers, facts or entire publications, or musical ability go mostly undetected in public schools. A child found mentally retarded by one test may be a genius by another.

As a result of protests from various researchers that ghetto children and children of immigrant parents were at a distinct disadvantage when it came to verbal aptitude, I.Q. tests were banned by the San Francisco and Los Angeles school boards in 1970.

Nevertheless, it is interesting to point out that we have been able to improve I.Q. scores for many of our clients through our TIM programming techniques.

We have also found that many other factors affect individual performance, including height, weight, rank among various siblings (with the firstborn seemingly enjoying distinct advantages in many cases), and the alphabetical order of last names.

That names do play a role in life cannot be denied. The selection of Neil Armstrong over a vast number of competitors as the first man to set foot on the moon was, to us, no coincidence. The name Armstrong was for decades associated with the all-American boy. After Arnold Palmer's lengthy reign as the leading male golf pro, the emergence, on the distaff side, of another Palmer, Sandra, as a habitual winner seems to be perfectly understandable.

Jackie Robinson was the first black baseball player to become a major leaguer when he joined the Dodgers in 1947. In 1974, another Robinson, Frank, also scored a unique first. The Cleveland Indians picked him as the first Black to manage a major league team.

Intelligence:

The more we study life, the more impressed we become with one outstanding phenomenon: *All people — regardless of education, age, race, nationality or religion — have intelligence.*

Given half a chance, and proper understanding, they can master any challenge or condition. People can perform functions ordinarily not expected of them.

Take the case of a youngster, age six, who drove home his father's car when the father was stricken by a heart attack. Or the 38-year-old woman who had never flown before, who took over the controls and safely landed a private plane after her pilot husband died of a stroke.

Intelligence of a highly individualized nature undoubtedly made possible the accomplishments of "uneducated" people such as the Fultons, Edisons, Wright Brothers and others. It also explains the success of Kate Smith, once one of the most popular singers in America, who never took a lesson in her life, and readily admits that she cannot read a note of music.

Professor William B. Shockley of Stanford University, a Nobel Laureate in Physics, has aroused much controversy with his contention that Blacks are inferior in intelligence to Whites because of genetic factors. We join the chorus of those disagreeing with him. Our reasons, however, are rooted in science rather than pious liberalism. Intelligence, we assert, is as ubiquitous as electricity. It is equally available to — or actually inherent in — all men and creatures. According to our deductions, the DNA — the molecule containing the information of inheritance — in every cell capable of replication records not the level of ancestral and individual intelligence but ancestral as well as individual concepts about one's own as well as others' intelligence. This hereditary concept accelerates or impedes the flow of intelligence like a resistor in an electrical circuit. Therefore, with the passage of time, and further advances in general enlightenment, we can predict the disappearance of racial differences in this vital aspect.

This development parallels another observation made by us in our paper on Mental Genetics. Consciousness factors are responsible for the gradual lightening of the skin pigment of Blacks and members of other races in contact with — or aware of — Whites. The resultant desire to be White will insure their looking like Caucasians in a few generations even without benefit of what was formerly called miscegenation. Explicable also in terms of consciousness is the birth to dark-haired, dark-eyed Jews facing extermination in Nazi-occupied Europe of blonde, blue-eyed children.

By the same token, we ascribe the gradual increase in height and weight of the average Japanese and Mexican to desire rooted in learning through personal contact, television or motion pictures. Biologists, physicians, and anthropologists have attempted to explain these changes in terms of improvements in diet. We refute this argument. Many contemporary youngsters consume, in the form of hamburgers, potato chips, and soft drinks, less protein, more starches and carbohydrates than their predecessors. The process involved here is, we assert, explicable in terms of the flow of impulses from the eye and the other sensory organs to the DNA via the afferent nervous system.

Intelligence in Animals, Plants:

In recent years it has become well known that creatures formerly considered unintelligent are actually highly intelligent. From the simplest cell to the highest organism, everything has been found to have intelligence.

Dolphins and porpoises that talk and sing, parrots that teach mutes to speak, dogs, lions and tigers that perform incredible tricks have become well known. Our own red-ear turtle, "Magoo," has learned to do push-ups and flip over on his back (supposedly impossible for a turtle).

That plants listen, respond, talk and sing in response to the human consciousness is now fully accepted. A grape ivy in our office, upon being threatened with removal in six months if it didn't cover a new trellis that had been installed in its pot, did so in half the time. A dying Boston fern revived upon being promised mention in this publication. As if angry at being ridiculed for its small size, a prayer plant has almost tripled in height and width, thus almost stealing the limelight from the other plants.

Even the fetus — and not the mother — decides when the time has come to be born. (Until recently, said Dr. Graham C. Higgens of Auckland, New Zealand, on February 11, 1975, researchers believed the mother played the dominant role.)

We already stated that cars, clothes, houses and all objects assume the owner's or occupant's consciousness. So do streets, cities and nations. They acquire their own personality. In the form of electrical activity, probably infrared in frequency, they retain all that has been thought, felt, said, and done by humans who may have left or died long ago.

Electrical instrumentation sensitive enough to determine what happened will, we contend, one day become available. The principle here is similar to that involved in infrared photography. It can take pictures of an airplane hours after it has left the runway.

All this boils down to an amazing fact: Nothing dies.

Events as Electrical Activity:

Man and everything he sees and touches consists of natural energy. This, as is well known, can neither be created nor destroyed. Therefore, technically speaking, every event is electrical activity which is as eternal as the atoms constituting it.

Just as gifted psychics today can "tune in" on events that are happening far away, so — we believe — one day will we be able to experience any given event in history — whether it is collective or singular in nature.

There is no death, except in concept. There is actually no time. In reality there is no space. The rapidly increasing speed of space and other forms of flight is proof that we are heading in this inevitable direction. We'll be "there" before we start.

An amazing unity links all to all. This explains the invisible bond we have already described between twins, between mother and child, husband and wife, benefactor and beneficiary, victimizer and victim, and all humans forming complementary units, even if they have never previously met.

Thus, we can readily see that, in this perfect universe, there can be no accidents. There is only law and order. Scientists may describe what they cannot understand as "atomic" or "genetic" mishap. Theologians may speak of "divine" errors. But all they see is their own concepts reflected back at them.

As Albert Einstein said, "God doesn't play dice with the universe."

Explicable only in terms of consciousness are many phenomena that are puzzling even to serious physical scientists. The social husband who assumes his wife's shyness a few years after marriage. The sober wife who starts drinking more than the mate or parent she formerly criticized for the same habit. The poor boy who becomes richer than the classmate he once envied. The healthy woman who becomes as sickly as the aunt she once resented because she had to care for her. Man's mental camera and tape recorder are ever at work, evening the score, eliminating differences. That's why things never stay the same. The consciousness of Manhattanites who moved West transformed the Los Angeles skyline into a modern New York. In such romantic cities as Paris and London, to the dismay of romanticists, centuries-old landmarks are being dwarfed by skyscrapers. American-style fried chicken and hamburgers are available on the Champs Elysees and the Ginza, while steak teriyaki can be had from Times Square to Main Street. Conversely, rural-type buildings and parks dot the big cities while the countryside, throughout the world, assumes a progressively more urban appearance. Similarly, formerly Capitalist countries become more socialistic. Communist nations manifest Capitalist characteristics.

History seems to repeat itself. This is easy to explain in terms of the total prevailing mind. When the movie *The Great Gatsby* was released in 1974, a wave of nostalgia swept the country. Men and women began to think, dress, sing, dance and cavort in the manner associated with the Roaring Twenties. The subsequent downturn of the stock market that year, therefore, did not really surprise us. Many investors were as panic-stricken as their 1929 predecessors.

The world is not becoming one. It already is one. It was ever one. This unity has scientific reality. Just as Drs. James Watson and Francis Crick, at England's Cambridge University, discovered the double helix as the structure of the DNA (deoxyribonucleic acid), the fundamental genetic material, so Dr. Roger Penrose, mathematical physicist at Oxford University, has come up with the twister theory. According to Penrose, twisters are like spirals. They are even smaller than atom components. In essence they are double helixes, too. And, for that matter, on a larger scale, socially, politically, economically, so is man intertwined with man. In the macrocosm, so are the galaxies.

Every atom within man's body or without is a miniature solar system, in which a variable number of electrons, neutrons and other particles revolve around the proton. By analogy, we may regard every human being as a sun around which are revolving, like planets, the people with whom he interacts. In the same manner by which the sun's light is projected onto the planets in the solar system, man's consciousness is reflected by the human planets he knows or encounters. Noteworthy is that every man, woman or child, in addition to being a sun, also represents as a rule several planets in solar systems revolving around other human suns. Changes in consciousness, like changes in sunlight, naturally must alter the attitude and behavior — or "light" — reflected back to the originator.

The United States was established because the Founding Fathers protested discriminatory taxation by King George III of England and other political abuses. Now many U.S. citizens accuse government on the federal and state level of the same practices. Consciousness factors, rather than malice or incompetence, are, we contend, responsible for this development. Similarly, millions of immigrants fled the same sort of shortages and restrictions in their home countries that now threaten to curtail the quality of the American way of life. Only courageous action, from the White House to Main Street, based upon a thorough grasp of the applicable mental factors, can reverse the deplorable trend.

The ecumenical movement, initiated by the beloved Pope John XXIII, in the early 1960's, followed by East-West summit meetings, reflects the trend toward unity in matters spiritual, political and economical.

The first edition of this book, published in 1959 and enlarged in 1961, inspired the so-called Consciousness-Revolution. As a result, the term "consciousness-raising" became a household word usually associated with Women's Lib. We therefore ascribe the unprecedented historic acceptance of women by Harvard, Yale, the service academies, and police and fire departments to consciousness factors. The same holds true for the growing incidence of female criminality (including attempted presidential assassinations), marital infidelity and other forms of conduct formerly considered exclusively male.

Other effects of consciousness are also evident. Some labor leaders have become as powerful, affluent and, sometimes, imperious, as the business tycoons they — or their predecessors — once denounced.

Changes in the weather in various parts of the world may possibly be attributed to the brain-recorded learning of immigrants and travelers from colder, more humid, or warmer regions. Thus we can predict that snow will one day fall in Los Angeles.

Gene-physics:

So far we have spoken primarily of consciousness. We now introduce our next topic — Gene-physics. It combines two of our "babies" into a highly useful aggregate. The first part of the word deals with Mental Genetics. It shows that, contrary to classical genetics, only one-third of the data encoded in the DNA pertains to biological inheritance. One-third pertains, we have found, to data about ancestral attitudes, lifestyles, personality factors, and key experiences. The remaining third is concerned with the individual interpretation of data about oneself and others.

Life Pattern Predetermined:

Just as man's physical build and other characteristics are determined before birth, so his total life pattern is predetermined, according to our deductions, by the same process. Like a robot, he obeys whatever program has been established in his cell nucleus. The starlight which he sees at this moment originated millions or billions of light-years ago. By the same process, the thoughts, words and actions he uses had their origin hundreds or thousands of years ago. Without this understanding, systematic, meaningful improvements are impossible.

Like a printed circuit designed and manufactured generations ago, the brain contains the instructions determining the manner and sequence of reactions by which one responds — calm, cheerful, angry or violent — to certain stimuli. Therefore, everyone may be regarded as normal considering his background. Only when man realizes this fact can he rid himself of pride, guilt, shame, futility or ignorance obstructing him.

We have found the makeup of the DNA responsible for other phenomena also. Children given up for adoption will tend to display, as they grow up, the alcoholism, criminality, and other characteristics of their natural parents or other elders rather than those of their adoptive parents who often are free of such habit patterns.

Moreoever, we have discovered what we believe to be the prime purpose of all human activity: *the purification, by collective and singular effort — whether conscious, subconscious or unconscious — of the DNA*. The need for children to assume the uncorrected hangups of their elders is tied in with this process.

The environment and the DNA, we have found, influence each other in a highly specific and so far totally unsuspected manner. Here again, TIM has proved to be revolutionary. We have learned to use it as an effective tool for shortcutting the evolutionary process. Consciousness is a key factor here.

On the universal scale, history will repeat itself until man learns the lessons it endeavors to teach him. The same holds true collectively and singularly. Longevity, health, prosperity and other blessings are earned by those families and individuals who have learned to apply properly and continuously the material we teach and use.

Precisely as in the case of physiological inheritance, certain personality and behavior traits are dominant in one generation and recessive in the next. Therefore, children often resemble grandparents more than their parents. We also found that peculiarities of mostly childless uncles or aunts are often encountered in an unwitting nephew or niece. Freud and his followers never noted these phenomena.

To enlarge, particularize and utilize this knowledge in a manner useful to ourselves, our clientele and every interested man, woman and child, has been the main thrust of our recent efforts. Some of these we reported in our paper on Mental Genetics. A descriptive volume on our discoveries along these lines will follow at a future date.

Our cherished goal is to have a world that lives by the example of crimeless Mitla (pages 60, 61), a world in which everyone will be like Joe Traub, a Yellow Cab driver in New York City, who lost his wallet containing $260 and got it back. A miracle? Perhaps, but one we feel he earned the right to. His brain record contained the appropriate information for he had previously returned an attache' case — unopened — to a man who had left it in his cab. He didn't know until the owner opened it that it contained $2,200 in cash. He had also once found a bundle containing $420 in dollar bills and made sure it was returned to the forgetful owner.

Judging from experiences such as these, plus many of our own with clients, our goal is within reach.

PART II

RAISE YOUR CONSCIOUSNESS

A. INTRODUCTION

The preceding discussion has introduced you to a subject matter so complex tht many books would be necessary to cover thoroughly each subheading by itself. Such elaborateness is not our intent at this time. You, we are sure, desire a simple, general explanation of principles, an understanding of which could help you raise your consciousness to a level where you may confidently expect better results from life and in your relations with others. This, we believe, we have given.

In Part I you learned that the chair on which you sit is an effect. Its cause was an idea in the designer's mind. To improve the chair, a change in the causative idea and blueprint is required. By the same token, your personal, marital, occupational, and social status are effects that cannot be improved without a change of the underlying consciousness.

To assure you optimum results in the shortest possible time, we recommend that you take the following ten steps after reading the related text:

1. Consider yourself a success
2. Make decisions
3. Love (or, at least, like) yourself
4. Love (or, at least, like) others
5. See the possible
6. Regard everything as good
7. Complete what you start
8. Live abundantly
9. Don't compromise
10. Don't tell a soul
11. Make no excuses
12. Assert yourself
13. Watch what you hear
14. Be patient

B. SUMMARY

1. CONSIDER YOURSELF A SUCCESS

When you belittle yourself, you tell your mind, "I am no good," or "I am a failure." Thereby you command your subconscious to produce more failures for yourself. Besides, others, who are your reflection, will think less of you. The remedy? Be a success!

First of all, what is success? One man may regard himself as a success when he can hold a job for six months. Another feels on top of the world in earning $20,000 a year. A third thinks he has "arrived" if a day goes by without an argument with his wife. Success, as you can see, is relative. It depends entirely on your point of view.

No matter how unsuccessful you may feel, you are at all times in a position comparable to a baby learning to walk. Now, you would not condemn this baby for crawling, falling, or stumbling. Each of these acts is a necessary, normal, natural part of learning to walk. If we call the baby's achievement of proficiency in walking a success, do we have the right to regard as failures its inevitable preliminary falls?

By identical means, in the process of becoming a better husband, salesman, housewife, or office manager, you go through the same universal pattern that leads from crawling to walking. Whatever your position relative to the baby's may be, if you keep trying and applying the principles discussed here you cannot fail to reach your goal. So, even in the act of failing you are a success. For you must fail successfully to fail at all. And failing, like stumbling or falling, is a part of success.

Before a missile is finally accepted by the United States Air Force, many of its predecessors had to blow up or fall short of their mark. Every successful sales transaction is usually concluded only after a number of turndowns, particularly in the early stages of a sales person's career.

Because your mind will add to what you are or consider yourself as being, concentrate on what you already can do well. Work on what you aim at becoming, while focusing on the achievements reflecting your competence. Dwell on the one sale you made last week, instead of lamenting the nine instances where your prospect said, "No." In reality, you have benefited in every case. You may have learned what not to do the next time or how to present yourself and your product more effectively.

Seen in this light, each one of your experiences, jobs, efforts is an important stepping stone in the direction of your goal. It actually is an integral part of it. Therefore, you are a success at all times.

From this moment on, learn to act like a success. Read about successful men in your field. Start to live in the consciousness of success. Associate with successful people. Concentrate on success until you think, speak, feel it. Refuse to be part of failure and negation in any way. With the "success" concept preceding all you do from now on, your mind will soon produce a corresponding upswing in your affairs (see Fig. 2).

2. MAKE DECISIONS

The ability to make decisions is **a vital prerequisite** to success. All of us make decisions in our mind every day. But the important thing to understand is that a decision is not a decision unless we *act* on it. Even if we do act, the marriage, investment, trip on which we have embarked may fail. The reason is simple. We have not been taught or taught ourselves to abide by, argue for, and believe in our decisions.

Our mind can produce results only in one direction at a time. The spirit within us, the highest or third dimension of our being, is always affirmative. It says, "I can." But it can flow freely, giving success to our endeavors, only if mind is in accord with it. Mind, from previous learning, can be for, against, or neutral. The body or action has no choice but to move in accordance with what mind has decreed.

Figure 2

EFFECT OF CONCEPT ON ADJUSTMENT

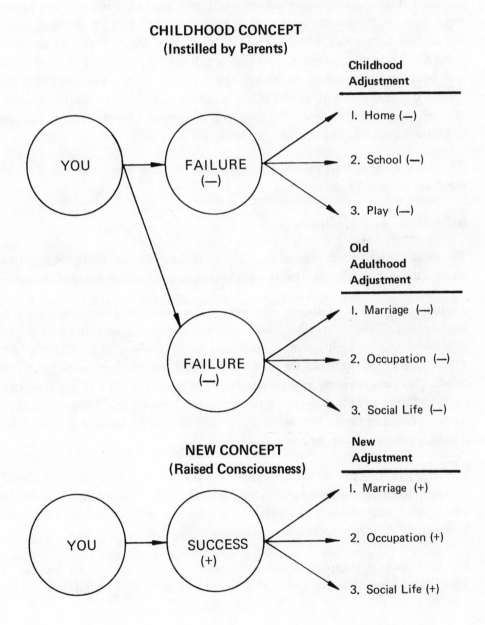

CHILDHOOD CONCEPT
(Instilled by Parents)

Childhood
Adjustment

YOU

FAILURE
(—)

I. Home (—)

2. School (—)

3. Play (—)

Old
Adulthood
Adjustment

FAILURE
(—)

I. Marriage (—)

2. Occupation (—)

3. Social Life (—)

NEW CONCEPT
(Raised Consciousness)

New
Adjustment

YOU

SUCCESS
(+)

I. Marriage (+)

2. Occupation (+)

3. Social Life (+)

Even when we are young, our mind is like an adult's. It needs a good reason for action, a reason that makes sense to us. If we were to tell ten-year-old Tommy to go outside, he would hesitate or not move at all. When we add that Jimmy, his softball teammate, is there, Tommy would exit quickly. But let us inform him that Mr. Smith awaits him, whose windshield he shattered the day before, and he might well refuse to budge. On the other hand, the news that Miss Jones, his teacher, was at the door would cause Tommy to react neither affirmatively nor adversely. The reason is he does not know whether she came to praise, condemn, or just visit him.

By analogy, it is imperative that we make up and keep our mind in the direction desired by us.

Indecision in Childhood:

The cause of our reluctance or inability to make decisions and abide by them stems from our childhood. It is there where confusion and indecision began.

Assume that Tommy's father tells him, "Yes, you can play ball," while his mother says, "No, you can't." Because Tommy likes to play ball, his desire will prompt him to be happy over the paternal approval. Now let his father's "yes" apply to lawn mowing, in contrast to his mother's "no" regarding the same chore. This time Tommy will lean toward the glum side. We all are by nature lazy, inclining toward the course requiring the least effort. None of us has to work at doing nothing. For us to spring into action, we need a desire, a good reason, a strong motive, or force.

The important point is that the same "yes" can arouse in us two directly opposite feelings, one joyous and one gloomy. The same holds true for the word "no." Our reaction depends entirely on the activity to which these two words apply. No wonder Tommy becomes confused.

His confusion is compounded further when his parents are inconsistent in approving his requests for permission to visit or play with friends at one time, while disapproving them at another time without a reasonable explanation.

As Tommy matures, this type of conditioning will cause his subconscious to be on a constant teeter-totter when it comes to deciding on a career, spouse, or other important matter.

Added to his confusion is indecision. Here is how it may start in us. One fine day we drop our baby spoon for the first time. Our parents smile their proud approval. Of course, we will expect further endorsement. Then one not-so-fine day, without previous warning, we are slapped or scolded for the same spoon drop that evoked praise before. From that moment on, we learn to be afraid of the consequence of some of our actions. In response to them, our mind may in later years produce psychological slaps in the form of failure, rebuff, or even severe physical harm.

Suppose you have to make a decision vital to you and are undecided. Perhaps an investment of $5000 is at stake or a lucrative job offer in a field new to you. As you realize that your indecision is not related at all to the alternatives presently confronting you but to your fear of the result of dropping your baby spoon or coming home late from school, you have already begun to destroy your childhood pattern of indecision. You can now apply the following three-step procedure:

How to Make Decisions:

a.   Weigh thoroughly all the pros and cons pertaining to your decision in accordance with your present level of understanding. Consider them as they appear to you. Contemplate the consequences of each. Do not make up your mind until you have carefully considered all the issues involved. When deciding on a purchase, trip, job, your old subconscious habit of settling for less than the best may trap you by causing you to feel inclined in this direction. Recognize this fact. Act in the opposite manner and raise your consciousness right then and there.

b.   Make your decision. Don't make a wishy-washy or contingent decision. But decide clearly, definitely, and finally. Then act in accordance with your decision. Without this vital action step, your decision is not a decision.

c.   Stand by your decision. After you have decided, your subconscious will bring up arguments against your decision. Others, reflecting your subconscious doubts or past pattern, may try to convince you of the folly of your course. Don't agree. Argue for your decision. Give yourself all the reasons at your command in favor of your decision. Close your mind to all negation. If you persevere, your decision will and must be successful.

You must learn to make decisions as systematically as you learn to walk. Even if, at first, your decisions turn out to have been wrong, primarily as the result of your past "wrong" pattern, don't give up. The fact that you have made a decision makes you a winner. In due course, as you persist, all your decisions will and must be right for you.

Before making decisions crucial for your future, train yourself by deciding on minor matters. Plan your schedule in detail for today. Make up your mind what you will wear tomorrow. Stick by your decision. Then proceed to decide on matters of increasing importance.

In this manner, you will achieve two important objectives:

a.   You discipline your mind by forcing it to dwell on what is desirable to you.

b.   By coordinating your mind and physical action in minor matters, you assure yourself of the ability to accomplish progressively more complex tasks.

One day, as you persist, you will be able to claim your mind. You will have bought your own self. Then you can achieve with ease such major goals as success in marriage, profession, or athletics.

3. LOVE (or, at least, LIKE) YOURSELF

Some people are prone to regard themselves as useless or unworthy. This, as a rule, is the result of conditioning by others. Parents or teachers may have expressed repeatedly their low esteem of the individual, whose subsequent behavior pattern developed in a corresponding direction. The subconsciously implanted belief in one's uselessness or evil nature must create, over the years, situations which will give him even more reason for condemning himself.

Also, from his father or mother he may have acquired the habit of comparing himself unfavorably against others. If the first standard for self-evaluation was a brother with superior scholastic or athletic achievements, the individual's mind will produce further reasons for lowering his self-esteem.

Nothing will be accomplished by telling someone not to feel guilty, useless, or inferior. We must make sense to him. Here is one way.

A man in search for a purpose in life may be compared with uranium. For billions of years, this metal lay hidden underground. The 1903 edition of Webster's Standard Dictionary called it "useless." In recent decades, however, science has made uranium a precious, highly useful element. By the same token, nothing in creation is without use.

Man, as a vital part of the whole, is no exception. Each one of us has a purpose for being. Sooner or later, we will and must discover it, whether by trial and error, necessity, sudden insight, or other means.

While babies do not discriminate against each other because of skin color or other reasons, men are taught to place themselves higher or lower than others. Inevitably, they will have their "comeuppance." Life is our great teacher. The U.S. Declaration of Independence proclaims that all men are created equal. Most people dismiss this as a pious untruth. Is a street cleaner, they scoff, equal to the President?

How to do it:

Here is how. Mathematics teaches us that two things equal to the same thing are equal to each other. Take a telephone and a lamp. How are they equal? The telephone is made for a use. The lamp also is made for a use. Because the two articles are equal to the same thing, i.e., a use, they are equal to each other. They are also equal in that they are unique. No other instrument can serve as a lamp except a lamp. The same holds true for the telephone. And there is a third reason why these items are equal. They both are exclusive. The telephone cannot be used as a lamp, while the lamp cannot serve as a phone.

The same arguments apply to man. We are all individuals. There are three billion people on earth, but nobody else has your set of fingerprints, your identical pattern of consciousness, your exact talents and abilities. You have a use, a uniqueness, an exclusiveness all your own. So don't sell yourself short!

Without you, an individual stone, the mosaic of life would be incomplete.

You may feel your age, education, race, nationality, sex, background, occupation is against you. Because you believe this, you may handicap yourself. Fortunately, man's prejudice against his brother is diminishing all the time. You can help accelerate this trend.

Age is Belief:

Consider age, for instance. During the Middle Ages the average human lifespan was 25 years. In some Asian countries, it still is only slightly above this level. Gradually, over the centuries, our longevity has increased to where we can expect to reach 70, 80 or even 100 years. This progress generally is ascribed to medicine, better nutrition, social conditions. In spite of the considerable contributions of these fields, the real reason for our increased lifespan is consciousness.

More and more, we see people live to a ripe old age, in full command of their faculties. When we consider the cases of many famous world figures, we can readily conclude that our bodies are able to retain their youthful vigor and beauty almost indefinitely except for the contamination of our subconscious by the belief in age and decay. You may have seen your grandfather limp along with the aid of a cane when he reached 60. Or a famous report on sex may have convinced you that at 30 you are "over the hill." Faithfully, your subconscious will produce the corresponding deterioration when you reach these age levels. At this very moment, however, certain groups of people in Tibet and elsewhere remain vigorous and productive, enjoying an average lifespan of 110 or more years, without benefit of diet, medicine, or a particularly favorable climate.

Remember, you are the commander-in-chief of an army of trillions of cells. Every thought you may think about aging or body deterioration these loyal soldiers will faithfully translate into physical reality. Conversely, they are just as capable of effecting for you the youthful appearance and capability you can choose, from this moment on, to retain or regain. When enough people become conscious of and learn to utilize these truths, early retirement, physical debility, and discrimination on account of age will become relics of the past. In summary, you are at the right age for a happy and successful life!

You may not like your height, weight, or appearance. This attitude, too, could stem from what others have made you believe about yourself. It may be entirely unjustified. Because any feeling of self-consciousness will cause others to reject or find fault with you, it is advisable for you to make yourself conscious of your assets, be they a pleasing personality or special capabilities. Also, take whatever action may be practical to modify or correct your physical condition.

Remember, your low evaluation of yourself is usually the result of what others have suggested to you and taught you to believe. This fact alone will help you see yourself in a new light.

Change Your Attitude:

You cannot change what you are and have done or experienced. But you can change your attitude about it. In the light of what you know and are today, you would probably act quite differently. This gives you no right to judge yourself by your standards of today.

You would not blame a baby for wetting his bed. At all times, he is doing his best according to his state of growth. The same holds true for you. You did what you did because it seemed right to you at the time and because of consciousness factors you did not understand then. Any other person in your shoes would have done the identical thing.

You have benefited from what has happened. Therefore, it was good. Avoid projecting into the future the errors, the heartaches of the past. Don't look back.

Today is a new day. Live it fully and joyously. You have grown from physical and mental babyhood into a maturity that will bring you greater peace and contentment because of what you did, because of what happened, and because of what you learned from it. Forgive yourself. Accept yourself. Like yourself. Respect yourself. Learn to love yourself. And most of all, learn to understand yourself!

Others, reflecting you, will have no choice but to show, by treating you better, how much you have progressed in this important direction.

4.   LOVE (or, at least, LIKE) OTHERS

Liking, let alone loving, others is extremely difficult for many people. This, too, is the result of childhood conditioning.
A baby, as a rule, seems to have no preconceived likes or dislikes until he learns about his environment and the people in it. But impressive evidence is accumulating in favor of the theory that a baby becomes aware of and reacts to his situation much sooner than was formerly believed. Accordingly, rebellion against his confinement in the mother's womb, the painful process of birth, and the smallness or clumsiness of his body may antedate any reaction to other persons. In some cases, fear of the unknown may take the place or be the cause of rebellion. This fear later may also relate to any real or imaginary menace that appears to threaten his security — be it a little brother or a dog.

Because of the mind's tendency to reproduce on a progressively larger scale our earliest learning or impressions, babies with these undesirable attitudes are bound to attract in later life ever more rebellion-arousing or fearful experiences. to themselves. The target of their rebellion may change, e.g., fear of dogs becomes fear of strangers, foreigners, economic uncertainties, but the causative feeling will remain the same.

Even when babies are apparently unaffected by conditions prevailing before, during, or shortly after birth, they soon learn to resent irregularity in feeding, parental inconsistency, unpredictability, and unkindness. This early resentment will grow, especially with additional instances of displeasing behavior by others.

Babies, having developed as yet no consciousness of their own, will react faithfully to the feeling of others, however carefully concealed it may be. In ignorance of how to hide their own reaction to adult love, indifference, or hate, they are pure reflectors. In this respect they are like animals.

Because his size, condition, and parental authority usually keep him from asserting himself, our baby will accumulate resentment like a boiler filling up with steam. Resentment will turn to hositility or outright hate. Eventually, as he realizes his inferiority at least during the formative years, he will feel frustrated, futile, or fearful of experiences even more undesirable than his past ones.

The very thought or sight of one or both parents will act as stimulus to an automatic chain reaction where resentment is experienced consciously, while all other feelings will follow through subconscious association. After many repetitions, the entire process may take place subconsciously.

Because our subconscious knows no time, no place, no person, the same resentment-hate-helplessness-frustration reaction will continue to plague our growing baby throughout life. It will repeat itself in association with teachers, employers, spouse, and others close to him. These persons are the effects, while the cause is a feeling or feelings connected with his parents.

By the law of action and reaction, resentment begets more resentment. As we express our resentment in word or action, others will merely retaliate. Should we try to hide our hostility or fear because of religious or other social conditioning, we would only fool ourselves. The hostile behavior of others toward us will reveal our true state of mind.

Unexpressed resentment, unless released, will in due course manifest in many ways. Here are three:

a. Physical illness
b. Hostility
c. Pretense of love and kindness

The first manifestation has been observed by us in many cases. Through entirely drugless means, combined with suggestion, the complete recovery of the victim was assured. The individual consciousness will determine the occurrence of cancer, ulcers, heart disease, or other conditions.

Hostility, on the other hand, is so strong in many people that they have difficulty in getting along with others. They may have frequent arguments at home, on their job, or wherever they may go. Often they get into fights. Even in cases where hostility is latent instead of overt, it merely awaits release as soon as the individual's consciousness attracts to him a suitable target for his resentment. Serving this purpose may be a situation as harmless as a traffic jam or a human scapegoat in the form of his wife, child, neighbor, or creditor.

The third manifestation of resentment, pretense of love and kindness, is the most common. Social restrictions force most people to repress their hostility. They are taught to hide their true feelings. Because they have not been shown or do not know how to sublimate their adverse emotions, they have become actors on the stage of life, concealing behind a mask of gentility and meekness a heart filled with hate, frustration, fear. But hypocrisy will be exposed.

Examples:

A married couple may be all smiles and kisses. Sooner or later there will be a violent blowup. Or a crippled, ill or hyperactive child will portray only too dramatically what is inside the parents. We have succeeded in helping bring about remarkable improvements in numerous cases of this type, considered hopeless by reputable physicians. Instead of working with the child alone, we started with the cause of his condition: the parents.

A man may appear to be exceptionally friendly and well adjusted until, under the influence of alcohol, a dismissal from his job, or a rejection by his best girl, he goes berserk. In less drastic cases, a salesman's prospects will turn him down. A housewife's neighbors will quarrel with her. Others will be shunned by those they wish to befriend. Inevitably, our true inner feelings, though actually unrelated to the people presently in our life, are reflected by our fellowman.

The cumulative buildup of unexpressed resentment that started with parents will attract to one, by sheer necessity, a socially acceptable excuse for its release on a mass scale. From the beginning of time, enemy nations, racial or religious minorities, political opponents have served this purpose. Especially stressed should be that resentment or fear is and was necessary on *both* sides for a clash to arise in the first place.

After each war or hate campaign, the causative collective hostility would subside, only to rear its ugly dragon head again as a new generation reached maturity and needed a release for its destructive emotions. The more repressive the parental behavior, especially in militant or autocratic nations, the more frequent the incidence of war or prejudice.

To change this pattern universally and assure a lasting peace for the world, we must learn, in the absence of leadership enlightened along these lines, to arrest the cause on the individual level. We must stop and convert resentments at their point of origin, i.e., before they become subconscious. This we can do through reasoning. For instance, we can convince ourselves that our boss or spouse is not our father or mother, that he actually means well, that his behavior is the result of his own pattern and our own expectation. We must reason this way until we feel peaceful and calm.

In time, this will produce into being a new understanding, followed by confidence in our ability to cope with life, especially as the improving behavior of others gives us more justification for proceeding along this path. At last, success or satisfaction will be ours (See Fig. 3).

Negative to Positive:

By thus replacing an undesirable chain reaction with a desirable one, you will form a new habit of being peaceful on the inside as well as externally. As you persevere, your relations with others will become progressively more enjoyable. In this manner, you not only benefit yourself but all with whom you come in touch. You will make a lasting and actually more effective contribution to world peace than would be possible through universal disarmament. For disarmament, an effect, cannot cure war which is also a mere effect.

By the same process, you could insure yourself against ever having cancer, ulcers, heart disease, or other sickness. If ill, you could help speed your recovery. For all physical conditions are effects, just as on the international scale the countries hostile to ours are effects. No sooner has medicine conquered one disease than another, so far unknown, disease is discovered. When mankind at large is taught this truth and the principles outlined in this document are applied, we can hope to enjoy permanent freedom from malady in any form.

Figure 3
ELIMINATION OF RESENTMENT

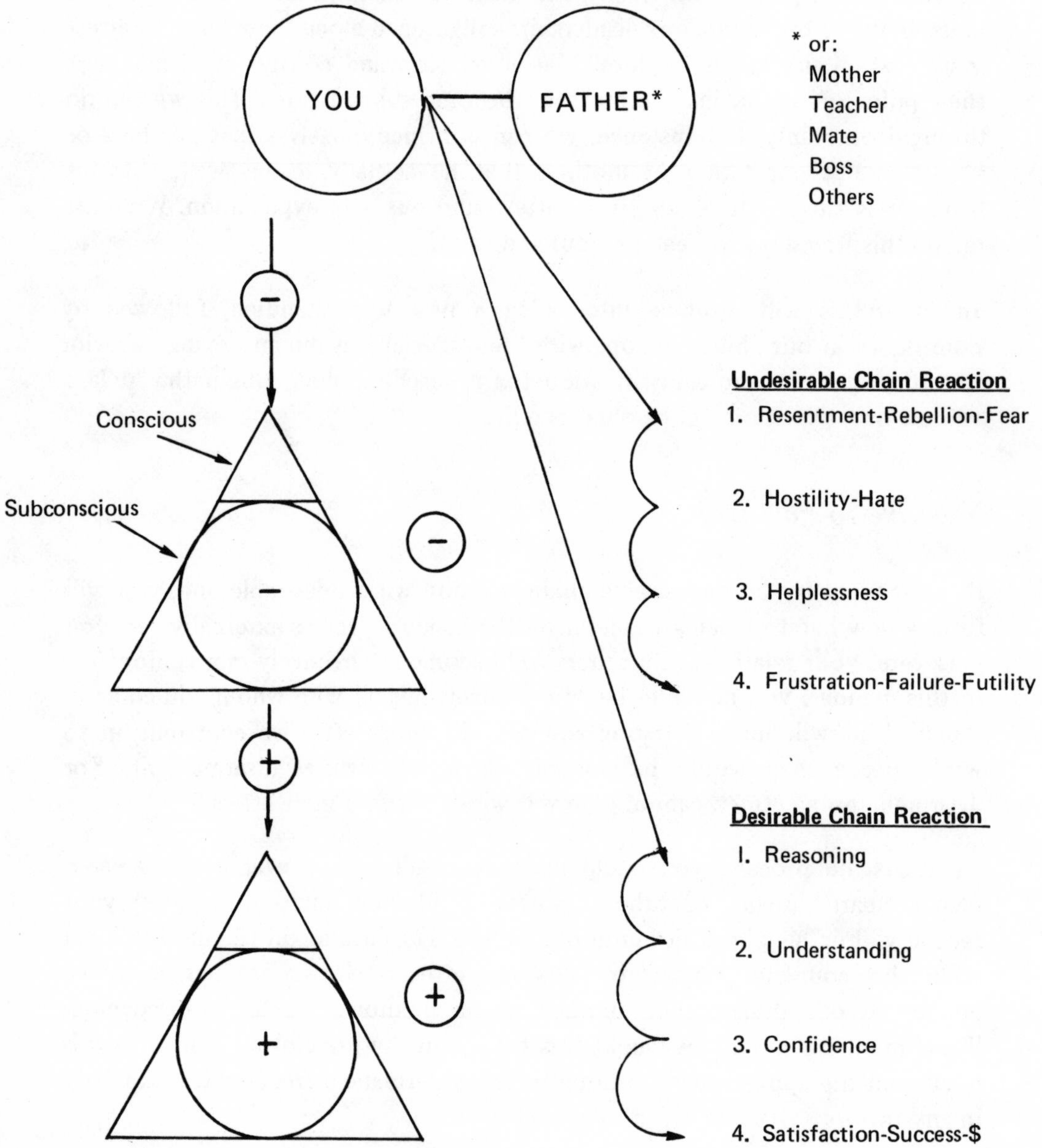

YOU

FATHER*

* or:
Mother
Teacher
Mate
Boss
Others

−

Conscious

Subconscious

−

−

+

+

+

Undesirable Chain Reaction

1. Resentment-Rebellion-Fear

2. Hostility-Hate

3. Helplessness

4. Frustration-Failure-Futility

Desirable Chain Reaction

1. Reasoning

2. Understanding

3. Confidence

4. Satisfaction-Success-$

Returning to you, you may regard your wife, partner, friend as uncooperative. Remember, the uncooperativeness you see reflects your inner belief that others don't play ball with you. Again, this concept started long ago. It may have seemed to you that your mother or brother went against your wishes. In reality, this may not have been true. We all, especially while young, interpret the behavior of others not objectively but as it appears to us. Subsequently, we will receive from others what our early and entirely subjective interpretation has caused us to expect.

As you realize that even in the act of apparently not cooperating, people actually do cooperate with your belief in noncooperation, you will soon feel much better toward them. Keep telling yourself, "Everybody cooperates with me." Before too long, you will reap results in the form of the understanding and cooperation you have desired since you were a child.

Consider Causes:

Besides, you may feel you cannot please your mate and resent him or her for nagging you. Consider the cause. It may be your childhood belief that you could never win the approval of your parents, no matter how hard you tried. This inability-to-please belief, if permitted to continue, could result in your incapability to earn a sufficient income, to do anything right, to satisfy sexually. In many cases, treated incorrectly and unsuccessfully as sexual impotence by physicians, this attitudinal factor is involved. Make yourself conscious that your spouse is merely an effect. Reverse the pattern by suggesting to yourself, "I am pleasing to my wife and everybody." Start by proving this to be true in little things first. Go on from there.

On the other hand, your mate may not please you. This could be a mere continuation of your childhood pattern of being dissatisfied with yourself, your parents, your home. When you reflect on this, your feelings about your marriage will change. He or she is not the cause of your feelings.

Remember, happiness comes not from having what you want to have, being what you want to be, or doing what you want to do, but from learning to like what you have, are, and do.

Your mind will add to your new feelings of satisfaction. Keep reasoning in favor of how lucky you are. Before long, you will have even more and better reasons to feel this way.

Many parents, fearing to lose the love of their children, will refrain from treating them with the firmness required for optimum results. In the process, both parties suffer. The parents lose their self-respect and the respect of their children. The youngsters, on the other hand, grow up without adequate preparation for the discipline of college, profession, and parenthood. Only he who has learned discipline himself can train others wisely.

A parent who really loves his child will lay down reasonable rules of conduct for him. He will demand obedience, outlining whatever punishment may be expected in case of failure to comply. This way the child learns early that he must earn the right to enjoy his privileges. He learns that whenever he gives he *must* receive. If the parent is firm, fair, and consistent in enforcing these rules, no resentment can arise. A child, who knows what is expected of him and why, will respect and love his parent.

Break the Pattern of Isolation:

Also, you may prefer being by yourself. You could rationalize by explaining, "People leave me cold." Look for the reason. As a child, you may have been ridiculed or rejected by your playmates. Even earlier, a little brother or sister may have taken your place as your parents' favorite. At least, that's how it seemed to you. You had not learned yet that nobody can actually take your place. He can only assume his own. Whatever the case may be, you became afraid of others. You learned to fear going out.

This fear, lodged deeply in the subconscious, may keep many salesmen from making calls, spinsters from getting married, employees from advancing. The more you sit alone, the more your rationalizing, conscious mind will give you reasons for remaining alone. It may tell you that the weather isn't good, the party to which you were asked is dull, or the prospects you were supposed to see aren't interested. All these reasons may not be true. Very likely, the real cause is your subconscious isolation pattern. If permitted to continue, it may lead to neuroses or diseases to keep you home.

To break this pattern, cultivate a new habit.

Go out. Associate with others, no matter how hard your subconscious may try to resist you. Reason with yourself. Expect acceptance, happiness, opportunity for personal growth from others. In the beginning, you will feel uncomfortable as you try to make friends. The very fact that you do feel this way is a good sign. For we feel at home only in what we know, be it loneliness, lack, or failure. Persist until what is at the moment uncomfortable to you becomes easy and natural. As you break your pattern of isolation in your social life, the beneficial results from your effort will make themselves known in your occupation and other areas of your being. Soon you will have a new and better life in every respect.

Observe how much friendlier people will react to you as you establish your new pattern of gregariousness. Now you can understand why certain actors, politicians, ministers have such a large following. They love people. And people must and do love them, in turn. Your age, your education, your experience, your appearance do not matter. It's what you feel about yourself and others that counts!

One word of caution. In the process of learning to like or love people, many have a tendency to let others walk all over them. They are afraid that by speaking up they might lose the affection or interest of those they wish to cultivate. As a result, they may accept advice they don't believe in, go on trips they can't afford, buy clothes they detest, waste time they could put to better use elsewhere, suffer treatment they resent.

Should your friend's advice strike you as good, thank him and take it. If not, realize that you alone know what is best for you. You don't have to be nasty. Be polite but firm. Make the other know that you appreciate his good intentions. Give him the right to be as he is, just as you claim your right to be yourself. Honesty is the best policy. In the long run, it will attract to you friends who will appreciate you, stick by you, and honor you.

In dealing with others, you can show them your love and respect by being:

    a.   On time and dependable in every way
    b.   Considerate
    c.   Truthful

They, in turn, will have no choice but to reciprocate.

A businessman complaining that his customers did not pay their bills on time was told to change his own habits of being late for appointments and of procrastinating in the discharge of his own obligations. To his delight, his customers started soon to pay him on time. They did not have to be asked or be informed of his changed habits.

In the final analysis, you get only what you give.

5.   SEE THE POSSIBLE

You know by now that your mind will produce results only in accordance with your belief and that you must give yourself a reason you can accept for your ability to attain your goals.

Suppose you wanted to walk a hundred miles. You have never done it before. But you have walked five miles at one time in your past. Your mind knows you can do this. Therefore, you must start from there. The reason you give your mind must be personal and true for you. As you walk further and further, thus building your consciousness step by step, you will in time attain your goal.

In similar fashion, the idea of making one million dollars may be too fantastic for your mind to accept at this moment. But your mind cannot argue when you make yourself conscious that you have earned or are earning five or ten thousand dollars a year. Gradually, you can raise your sights.

Every time you say, "I can't" or "It's impossible," you decree a failure for yourself. Your "can't," spoken lightly in connection with some relatively harmless act, such as going to town, will sink into your subconscious and combine with all your previous "can'ts" to return to you at a time when you least expect it. In this manner, you can lose sales, pay raises, marital opportunities.

We all have been conditioned by our culture, parents, schools to accept as true certain absolute premises. In the process, we have often been fooled. Little Tommy, having learned to walk, won't stop to remind himself, "I can walk." He knows he can. Should he fall and break a leg, a doctor rushing to his side will tell him, "You cannot walk." Taught not to question a medic's authority on health matters, Tommy will accept his verdict as final. What he does not know is that at this very moment there are Eskimos and cannibals moving about on broken legs. They have never learned that this is impossible!

Furthermore, we may have been taught the impossibility of being healthy without a balanced diet, or of surviving certain diseases. Or that small, middle-aged women cannot lift heavy loads. But, as the examples in Chapter A (Part I) indicate, what is "possible" or "impossible" depends entirely on our individual consciousness.

Great, indeed, is he who has an imagination unrestrained by the knowledge of facts. Because his mind will produce what others call miracles. But just as great, if not greater, is he who uses his factual knowledge wisely and steadily to push back the frontier of his limitations.

To Bring About Desired Changes:

Because you cannot readily wipe out the "can'ts" you have accumulated in your subconscious over the years, it is difficult for you to say "I can do this or that," especially when you cannot give your mind a logical reason why your negative experience pattern need not repeat itself. But you can start right now to bring about the change you desire. Instead of declaring, "I can't go to town," say "I can go, but tomorrow will be better for me."

Your mind may not be ready as yet to "buy" completely your affirmation that you are a success. However, it will not reject your statement, based on your previous conditioning, "I simply cannot fail" or "I simply cannot lose." Thus, you are converting a negative into a positive.

For everyone who says, "No, it's impossible," there is someone who asserts, "Yes, it can be done," and goes ahead and does it. The very fact that you have something to sell is proof that there is a buyer somewhere. There is no problem without a solution, no need without a fulfillment.

By reasoning and acting in accordance with these principles, you will soon be in the habit of attaining the goals you, in ignorance, have put out of your reach so far.

6.   REGARD EVERYTHING AS GOOD

Because as children we were taught to view one act or thing as good and another as bad, our adult world reflects the same duality of standards. The result is frustrating for most of us, to say the least. Inconsistency in our values produces inconsistency in our feelings and experiences.

Specifically, dissatisfaction with your job makes unavoidable even greater dissatisfaction in your next position. The mind is impartial. It records in the brain your feelings or judgments and gives you more reason, pro or con, for feeling the way you do. Instead of telling yourself that you are wasting your time or that your job is beneath your capability, realize that you are acquiring valuable experience and proficiency. See yourself as being right for the job and the job as right for you. Don't stop reasoning until you have made sense to yourself. This way you are bound to attract more favorable employment opportunities. You have broken your old pattern of frustration.

To enjoy a happier future, we must learn to change our attitudes. You may have been taught to condemn others because of their selfishness. Let us see whether selfishness is really bad.

Consider the little peach seed. Planted in the ground, it must gather moisture and minerals from the earth to survive. As it becomes a sprout, it competes with other plants for nourishment not only from the soil but also from the sun and air. After successfully battling for life, taking and taking all the while, our peach seed will finally become a tree. Now, at last, it can start to give. But its first yield is meager enough. One tiny peach or two may comprise the first crop. After this first act of unselfishness, our tree becomes even more selfish. Deeper down into the ground bore its roots for more water and food, while its branches stretch higher and farther for more light and air. Slowly but surely, our selfish little peach seed has become a mighty tree, bringing forth thousands upon thousands of peaches year after year. The seeds from this fruit, in turn, will produce millions of peach trees and billions of more peaches in the long run. Without the selfishness of the first seed, such bounty would be impossible!

On the other hand, had our peach seed decided to be unselfish and let other seeds deprive it of its rightful share of whatever was necessary for growth, its yield would be a few scrawny peaches at best.

Seen in this light, you will certainly agree that it pays to be selfish. Selfishness is not necessarily bad.

Don't fret over who or what bothers you. Remember, even the most precious pearl would have never come into being without an oyster's irritation. When you blow up against another or he against you, smile — at least inside. Volcano eruptions produce the flow of lava which makes the most fertile soil on earth. Therefore, you will make your progress after such an occasion.

The Purpose of War:

All right, you concede. But what about war? As we showed you in Chapter 4, even this condition has its purpose. Furthermore, reflecting on World War II for example, it is easy to see that its long-range benefits outweigh by far its detriments. The birth of the United Nations, the industrialization of under-developed countries, the democratization of others, the greatest prosperity ever known to man, measures to wipe out genocide, illiteracy, disease, starvation — all these events benefiting billions of people resulted from the last global war. By 1957 alone, atomic energy used for medical purposes had saved many more lives than were destroyed by the A-bomb in Hiroshima and Nagasaki.

What about sickness? Our preceding discussions have shown the usefulness of this state as an expression of consciousness. Its very existence causes the search for a cure and a better understanding by medicine of the human body. Also, our days of disability make us appreciate the blessings of good health, just as a slum district serves as a measure for the beauty of a modern city. Because it enables us to discern the pleasant or desirable and instigates effort toward mankind's progress, what we call evil actually has a great purpose. In reality, therefore, it is also good.

The moral? Don't condemn anyone or anything. Don't join others in condemning anyone or anything. Because your subconscious knows no person, it will apply to you whatever you say or think about others. Your words, "He is a fool," will be translated into, "I am a fool," and backfire on you in the future.

At this moment you may recall many instances from your past that you once deplored but have come to see as blessings. The loss of a job, instead of ending your career, may open the door to greater opportunity.

Others may have cheated you. In righteous anger, you blamed and cursed them. Meanwhile, you may have changed your mind about them. Indubitably, your own consciousness of loss or fear was at least partly responsible for what happened. All this has taught you a great lesson, making you better and wiser.

From ignorance you have graduated into understanding. Out of what seemed evil came great good, just as the destructive use of atomic power brought about its application to peaceful purposes. Although once you were a child and are, physically at least, an adult now, you have remained the same person at all times. By the same token, all things grow from what seems evil into good. Because, actually, they have ever been this way. In the final analysis, all things are good.

Taxes and prices may have risen, but so has your ability to pay. Besides, in spite of what the pessimists have predicted for decades, we all enjoy more abundance, comfort, opportunity than ever before.

For the sake of your better consciousness, make yourself aware of what is good about you, your wife, your life. Instead of calling your memory poor, concentrate on the many things you do recall with ease. Tell yourself, "I have a good memory." Strive to recall more material all the time. With patience, you will and must succeed.

Law of Action and Reaction:

The law of action and reaction prevails in all dimensions of our being. Because the brain groove you cut today in the act of belittling others, if only in thought, must attract to you criticism from persons you may not even know as yet, enlightened self-interest dictates that you become more charitable toward others. Needless to say, by the same process, your actions, be they charitable or criminal, must return to you in kind.

This holds true also universally. Even hurricanes and forest fires (Smokey the Bear notwithstanding), despite their momentary disadvantages, have long-term necessity and benefits that were previously unsuspected. By the same token, you had involvements, associations and experiences you and everyone you knew condemned as foolish, wasteful or even harmful. In the long run, however, they turned out to be blessings in disguise. They taught you the most, making you prudent, wiser and immune against repetition. The same holds true for some of your past attitudes and actions. They may have created hardship for you as well as others. As a result, you were impelled — or you have now decided — to modify them. You don't have to be a behavioral scientist. Concentrate on what we and your own common sense have shown you. And watch your excellent results.

By applying these suggestions, only good will come to you. You won't have time for worry. You will have too much fun enjoying life, its blessings, its wonders.

7. COMPLETE WHAT YOU START

Most people dream big dreams, but few realize them. One of the major reasons for this failure may not be lack of intelligence, ability, or effort, but a habit formed in childhood.

Parents or teachers may have interrupted them in the middle of games, fun, and other activities important to them at the time. Later, they could have been forced to quit school prematurely or to give up a promising position. As a result, their subconscious was conditioned into a pattern of noncompletion.

Years later, this pattern will keep them from achieving their life goals. Either another person or an obstacle beyond their control will act as the disrupting agent. Or they themselves, controlled by subconscious habit, will commit an act, make a decision, perform inadequately to assure their failure.

Often another cause underlying such undesirable behavior may be ascribed to parental influence. A child may have been taught that the things he wanted most, i.e., candy or a bicycle, were bad for him. Conditioned this way, he will continue to reject what might be to his advantage.

As a rule, a member of this group will have a good excuse for his action. He might say, "I just couldn't stand this job any longer" or "There was no opportunity for advancement." When breaking off his engagement to the girl of his dreams, he may explain, "Margie and I have nothing in common." Later, he will berate fate or himself for his folly without realizing that his own subconscious habit pattern was the cause.

A man may have been conditioned to believe he had no right to marry unless he was a success. Success, to his parents, meant money. Since he had no money, he rejected his fiancee without realizing that he responded to subconscious factors. Similarly, one of our female clients was conditioned to prefer a political career to marriage by her father, who felt that his own marriage had kept him out of politics. As a result, she subconsciously caused the breakup of her marriage until she was shown the cause by us, after several psychiatrists had failed to do so. She disassociated herself with her father's attitude and became a happy marital partner.

Precisely as the man given a post-hypnotic suggestion to sing a song will explain his performance with a reason entirely unrelated to the actual subconscious cause, i.e., the hypnotist's command, so our reasoning mind will rationalize our subconsciously caused actions in terms that are usually without foundation of fact.

Because the pattern established by our mind is like a bed channeling the flow of a river from its source to the ocean, forceful action is required to assure its diversion into a more desirable direction.

Therefore, you should start by focusing yourself to complete everything you do. Begin with minor tasks, like writing a letter or mowing the lawn. Finish whatever you have permitted to go uncompleted up to now. Complete it as quickly as possible. Always do what you say you will do. Even in the act of dressing yourself, don't let anything or anyone interrupt you.

As you teach your subconscious that you mean business and refuse to accept disruption any longer, it will become your loyal servant by helping you complete automatically any project, no matter how large, you may have in mind.

8.   LIVE ABUNDANTLY

Most people dwell on how little money, time, energy, luck they have. In this manner, they are creating a prison for themselves, from which they will find it progressively more difficult to escape. When their investments are unsuccessful or an expected pay raise does not come through, the fault may not lie with their realtor, broker, or boss, but with their own words, "I'm always broke."

The traffic jam in which you were caught last week while en route to that important engagement did not happen by accident. Your oft-repeated words, "I don't have time," may have been to blame.

Instead of complaining about owning so little, make yourself aware of how much cash you actually do have, even if it is only one dollar. Look at it. Feel it, let it lie around the house so that your mind cannot argue when you say, "I have so much money I must push it aside to get at my shirts." Or books or papers. By this method, you will put your mind to work for you. Its multiplicative powers will increase your supply of cash with absolute certainty.

Constant focusing on your debts will, of course, have the reverse effect. Few people know what they do to themselves when they say, "Every time I pay a bill, there is another to take care of." They are merely insuring themselves against ever having money for purposes other than the reduction of their liabilities. Therefore, their mind must create more and more debts to keep them from enjoying their money for better living.

To avoid the need for constantly coping with financial obligations, abolish the word "pay" from your vocabulary. Replace it with "give." Whenever you take care of a bill, see yourself as a philanthropist providing employment, good health, pleasure, and education for many. As you give, so you must receive. Teach yourself to say, think, and feel, "For every dollar I spend, I always receive two." This will change your pattern of always spending more than you take in, a habit so universal that it has resulted in a steady rise of the individual and national debt. Adopted on a wide enough scale, this novel practice could do more for balancing the federal budget than radical economy measures devised by the world's best economists who, by focusing on deficit, would merely help increase it.

Become conscious of abundance in everything. If you cannot accept the belief that you have a lot of money, dwell on the billions of dollars owned by the richest men in the world. Put yourself in their shoes; learn to feel, think, and act like them. The gross national product of the United States during the current year will exceed $1,500,000,000,000 (1½ trillion dollars). You certainly cannot dispute that you own and benefit from at least some of this tremendous wealth. Apart from money, there are seventy trillion cells in your body. At this very moment you are inhaling billions of molecules of air. Note the many clouds, the hundreds of millions of stars in the sky.

Surround yourself with abundance. Instead of purchasing one item at a time, buy several bars of soap, cereal cartons, rolls of toilet tissue, handkerchiefs. Don't be stingy when buttering your bread, filling your plate, going out. Build up your wardrobe. Gradually acquire a few items you have formerly denied yourself. Prove to your mind that at least a portion of your money goes toward better living for you. Soon it will provide more for this worthy purpose.

Ever since the start of the money system, man has considered prices too high. This has driven them ever higher. Instead of seeing everything as costing you a lot, make yourself aware that you always receive so much for so little. When you consider the service, convenience, quality, and quantity available to you at most stores or restaurants, you may readily agree with this suggested change in attitude. Before too long, its adoption will pay off in further benefits to you, including more quality and quantity. This attitude can stop inflation, at least for you.

Lack Patterns:

If you don't have time for fishing, travel, or writing, realize it is you who is responsible. You let yourself be dominated by the lack-of-time pattern, closely related to the lack-of-money, lack-of-everything malady so prevalent in our culture. It is up to you to reverse the trend, for yourself at least. Decide to take time right now. Learn to give time to yourself, precisely as you once learned to give it up or waste it. If you gain only one minute a day to begin with, it's a start in the right direction. As you persist, your mind's ability to multiply will assure you of ever more time for the things you always wanted to do.

As a result of conscious or unconscious imitation of your parents, you may have acquired the habit of working too hard. This makes it extremely difficult for you to relax and have fun. Because your subconscious will resist any effort to change, it may try to convince you through conscious thoughts that having fun will keep you from success. Or it may create in you guilt feelings at the very idea of desisting from your incessant strife to provide adequately for your family.

By understanding these principles, you will find it relatively easy to avoid being fooled. Make good sense to yourself. You have a right to laugh and play. Your mind and body need a change from the old routine. If your mind knows only work, that's all you will have in the future. But by learning to take time out for fun, you will free yourself step by step from your rat race of habit or your false fear of insecurity. Tell yourself, "The more I play, the more money I make." Eventually, as you balance your life, you will feel much better. This will lead to improvements on every score, including your income.

Money will lose its power over you as you see yourself as the center of a vast and constant exchange. Do not hoard it. Reward others for their services to you. Tip freely. Take care of your bills cheerfully. Do not ask others to do anything for you without pay, unless you want to give your services free of charge. As you use it fearlessly, money will become your servant, giving you freedom, pleasure, and confidence in your ability to accomplish more than you ever dreamed of in the past.

Free Your Subconscious:

Don't depend on money alone. In this manner, you free your subconscious to bring you what you want by one of many other ways. One of our clients believed himself incapable of getting the new house he needed for his growing family because of a low salary. Only a few weeks after we convinced him that his problem could be solved even without a greater income, he was asked by fellow investors to occupy and manage a large new home purchased by them for future income purposes. In exchange for his and his wife's services, his monthly rental was reduced by half.

Perhaps as a youngster you were deprived by someone else of the money you had earned and saved. This way, your subconscious learned, "I cannot have money." Subsequently, in spite of your efforts to succeed, it loyally prevented you from making sales, getting promoted, or accumulating money by creating an accident, lawsuit, illness, and other emergency just when you seemed to have attained security. In such a case, it would be wise for you to make a special effort to save for a while until your subconscious accepts your constantly reiterated self-suggestion, "I can and do have money."

You may be in the habit of complaining about how little sleep you get or how tired you are. This also may be due to unconscious learning. The more you dwell on your small supply of energy, the less will be yours in the future.

Just as a pain in your body requires more concentrated energy than when you are well, so complaining about your listlessness will merely intensify it. Regardless of how low you feel, you do have a certain amount of energy in your body. Concentrate on it. Talk about it. Use it to exercise, to move about. Feel it surging through your muscles, veins, and entire being. Glory in it. The more freely you spend what you have, be it money, time, energy, ideas, the more your mind will supply for you. Like several of our clients pronounced hopelessly anemic by their physicians, you will soon have at least as much vitality as your most dynamic friend.

Instead of focusing on what may ail you, concentrate on the health you are enjoying elsewhere in your body. Don't dwell on your problems. Regard them as challenges that measure and increase your capability. Don't harp on what irritates you, but delight in what is pleasing to you.

For your subconscious, there is no tomorrow nor yesterday. All it will ever know is the here and now. As you make yourself aware that you are fulfilled with all the money, energy, intelligence you need for this one second, you will produce more fulfillment into being for the seconds that lie ahead. You can live only one second at a time. Make sure that each one becomes more glorious and satisfying for you.

Picture in front of you a patch of weeds on one hand and a rosebush on the other. The weeds are symbolic of your bills, troubles, ill health, reverses. The roses represent your happiness, good fortune, money, health. Every time you think of or talk about the undesirable, visualize yourself as watering the weeds and killing off the flowers. But as you dwell on your assets, you give growth and beauty to the roses, thus exterminating the weeds.

We already know what you will do from now on.

9. DON'T COMPROMISE

Most people have been conditioned or trained themselves to settle for less than the best. Like Mark in Chapter B (Part I), they will let themselves be shunted aside by others as a matter of course. Since they had to be satisfied as children with substandard food, clothing, education, their mind will continue to keep them in a state of inferiority. The places, the people, the circumstances in our life may change, but subconsciously we remain in the home where we grew up.

When a man like Mark insists on the best table in a restaurant, his subconscious may try to argue him out of his decision, either directly or through others around him, by insisting that he settle for a lesser seat. When he intends to buy the finest suit in a store, his inner enemy may cause him to feel guilty by whispering, "This is too much money to spend on yourself."

Insist on the Best:

If you are another Mark, don't give in. Insist that you are entitled to the very best. Train yourself to get the best in life by starting to give yourself the best in relatively minor matters. If you were to wait for circumstances or your money supply to be just right, you would never progress. Instead of waiting until you think you can afford the trip to Europe you always wanted, take a weekend cruise or a brief vacation to get into the travel habit. After repeated efforts along this line, your mind will believe you when you say, "I travel often. I can and will go to Europe." The subconscious will help you get there automatically. In due course, if you keep on trying, you will have the money for your own Grand Tour.

If you think you cannot afford to eat out or what you like every night, start by dining out at least once a week. Break your lack-consciousness by not settling for hamburgers on that evening. Go first class. Go to the finest restaurant in town. Get the steak you like. You may spend a few dollars in excess of your old norm, but your action will buy a million dollars' worth in beneficial reactions which will change your feelings of guilt at your extravagance. This will make it possible for you to have more opportunities for feeling even better.

By improving, in similar fashion, your standards of housing, transportation, and recreation, you will raise your consciousness substantially. But a word of caution is indicated here. If your mind has been in the habit of providing a "beer" standard of living for you, it cannot be expected to adjust to your desired "champagne" taste overnight. Because it may have idled along on a $500-a-month budget, your mind needs a systematic step-by-step push upward before it can assure you the $2000-$3000 or more a month you would like.

Also, if you have lived on a regular paycheck so far and are without substantial savings or other assets, a sudden switchover to the status of a commissioned salesman may be as unwise as diving into icy waters without cooling off first. Learn to sell part-time until your confidence in your sales ability has grown sufficiently. Then give up your job and sell on a full-time basis.

The beautiful truth is this: It is just as easy for your subconscious to supply you with a million dollars as with ten. All that is needed is proper conditioning.

Go First Class Everywhere:

By learning to go first class everywhere, you will train your mind to assure you commensurate treatment in your occupation, social life, and even at home. You can hold out for any salary or thing you want. Once your subconscious learns you will not compromise, it will give you the very best.

Every time you settle for a poor theater seat or second-class merchandise, you tell yourself, "I haven't got money," and you will have less the next time. Whenever you permit others to push you around, you signal your subconscious, "I am not important." Don't blame others if you are treated even more dismally in the future. By the same token, in walking all over others, in lying or failing to keep your promise to them, you order your subconscious to let people do the same to you in the days that lie ahead.

Now you know how to acquire dominion over your physical environment. As you realize that you need not depend on outsiders for your ideas, wealth, time, and opportunities, you will grow in confidence. The resultant feeling of self-sufficiency will free you forever of all fear of having to be at the mercy of others or circumstances.

10.   DON'T TELL A SOUL

One of the secrets of success is that you must learn to keep a secret. More precisely, you should mark every project that's really important to you "off limits" to others — especially those who love you or know you well.

This probably sounds cruel or paradoxical. Your family and friends, you may feel, are rooting for you. They should be the first to know what you are up to, because they obviously wish you well. Therefore, it's easy to understand why you can hardly wait to tell them about your new project or idea — its every feature and aspect, pro and con. One of life's real pleasures, the saying goes, is sharing one's cherished dreams with friends.

Yet, nothing can be more dangerous when it comes to establishing a new pattern for yourself. At least, that's what our experience with thousands of cases has taught us. For you are not dealing with a routine matter. It cannot be treated lightly. You are waging war. War against old habits and concepts pertaining to yourself, rooted in your own brain and that of everyone who knows, loves or hates you. And without a leakproof security system, most wars are lost before they start.

You are the commander-in-chief, responsible for your long-range strategy and step-by-step tactics. You are also the security chief, charged with anticipating, exposing and, if need be, executing (or, at least, eliminating) spies. And, finally, you are the soldier carrying out the plan you yourself have conceived. Now and then, you are permitted to lose a battle. But, in the end, you must win the war.

Poor security chiefs cannot be tolerated. They must be replaced. With reference to you, this means a new and better system has to be devised.

Example:

This is precisely what we did for Carl, a real estate salesman who became one of our clients. A commander-in-chief, security chief or soldier doesn't have to rely on his own wisdom. He can have advisers on his staff. But they'd better know their business, including his strong points as well as his weak ones. Our results, in Carl's and many other cases, prove that we qualify.

Carl had piled up a mediocre performance record before coming to our office and seminars. He learned to understand and raise his consciousness, set goals and earn good money. As he became aware of his potential, he raised his sights. He met the owner of one of our city's leading hotels and offered to list the property for him. The proprietor seemed interested. Our client and student beamed. He already could see himself receiving a commission greater than his entire earnings up to that time. Before he consulted with us, he went to lunch with three members of his profession and, as the saying goes, spilled the beans. He let them in on what he considered his good fortune.

A few days later, to his dismay, he learned that the owner had changed his mind. There was no deal — at least with Carl. Upon his request, we decided to analyze the facts. We knew two of those who had been present at lunch when Carl had announced the impending sale. One told us he was certain it would fall through. Why? "Carl's too green," he said. "He hasn't got what it takes." The second, an analytical broker, advanced another reason for Carl's failure. "You can't rely on that guy," he explained. "He's never on time. Also, he isn't trustworthy."

Mentally, we showed Carl, these two were pulling against him. They saw him as he was before being re-educated by us. So did a substantial portion of his brain record. His new conscious efforts and pattern were as yet too weak to prevail against such opposition. The influence of those adverse concepts sufficed to stop the deal. Thus he lost the electrical tug-o-war that always rages between and around those about to break an old pattern in favor of a new one.

We didn't know Carl's third luncheon partner. But there was no doubt about what he thought of Carl. As soon as the fateful lunch was over, he raced to his office, called the vice president of a large hotel chain he knew and another potential buyer. Then he submitted a business-like proposal to the hotel owner, pointing out in action the advantages of dealing with him instead of Carl. He got the listing and made the sale.

Carl learned his lesson well. He followed our advice and let his subsequent results rather than his initial enthusiasm speak for him. After a while, his friends, associates and even those he didn't know saw the truth. He had become a new man. There was no doubt now about his effectiveness. He consummated sale after sale. Eventually, his sales led not only his own agency, but practically the entire region. It was then that he could emulate the great Babe Ruth who pointed toward the sky to indicate the trajectory of a vitally important home run. The expectation of others was now in his favor. They helped him to achieve his progressively more ambitious goals.

We trust we have made our point. When it comes to oral support, your mother, granddad, Aunt Sue, mate, golf partner and bartender undoubtedly are all for you. But you don't know what they really are thinking about you. For that matter, often neither do they. At least, it's very likely that they don't suspect the effect their concepts may have upon you. "Poor Al," they may think, "doesn't he know that with his high-school grades, he can't be more than a janitor?" Or: "No one from our family has made it big." Or: "How can Jane think Jim Jones will marry her? He's bound to see right through her bluff!"

In such vital matters as business, romance, sports or what have you, learn from the wise hen. She cackles only after laying an egg. In effect, she tells the world around her, "I'm a success. Just look at what I've done!"

Silence is golden. It also is psychic as well as physical power, measurable in the precise terms of physics. Thought unexpressed contains more energy units than after it is dissipated by speech or co-mingled with doubt or outright opposition. Especially when backed by continuous, determined action, it represents a practically "irresistible force." To make sure it doesn't encounter adverse opinion, the mental equivalent of the proverbial "immovable body," keep your mouth shut.

Let your achievements be the jewels that adorn the crown on your victorious head.

11.   MAKE NO EXCUSES

The habit of making excuses probably originated with Adam. Even if you don't believe in the Bible, the story makes a vital point. When asked by God why he had eaten of the forbidden fruit, Adam didn't beat around the bush. (Or the tree, to be technical.) He simply blamed Eve. "She gave it to me," he said. Mind you, she didn't twist his arm. She just handed it over to him. In the long run, his excuse didn't do him a lot of good. In fact, no good at all. He was kicked out of Paradise anyway. For the naked truth was undeniable. He had done what he wasn't supposed to do. And it couldn't be negated by billions of the most carefully conceived and skillfully presented excuses.

So it is with contemporary man. Excuse-making is still rampant. Over the centuries, it has become a refined art. Even children have become amazingly adept at making up the most ingenious alibis. If you are a parent or a teacher, you undoubtedly know. If you are still a child, you also know. The stories that have been told to explain tardiness, noncompletion or omission of homework, unauthorized behavior, could make an endless comedy series on television and stagger the imagination of even the most jaded humorist.

In case you are a sincere adult exasperated by this sort of juvenile deception, you'll probably demand that teachers instruct children to stop blaming their delays on accidentally disconnected radio alarms or missing maternal oil credit cards, and their study failures on sick dogs, brothers who wouldn't switch off the family television set, or faulty air conditioning.

If you are a teacher, you'll indignantly refuse to take the blame. You will insist that the parents are responsible. Didn't they get the first crack at Johnny's and Mary's impressionable brains? Let's face it, you're right. But we'd like to point something else out. *You have just made an excuse.* "If those parents had done their job right, we teachers wouldn't have any problems with the little darlings." That's what you are saying. Conversely, the parent who says, "It's not mine but a trained teacher's job to make my youngster face the music," has also made an excuse.

The Reflection Principle:

We have already explained the reflection principle. Accordingly, parent and teacher reflect each other in attempting to shift the burden on the other's shoulders. The parent's attitude and words indicate what the teacher thinks and feels, just as the teacher's attitude and words reflect the parent's inner processes.

The situation is further complicated by the fact that many parents are professional teachers, or *vice versa.* When such an individual says the parents are to blame, he acknowledges his own responsibility for what is happening. That part of his brain record which pertains to his parent status duly registers this fact. It records that he has done — or is doing — something wrong.

Consequently, he must and will attract people and situations reflecting this judgment. In other words, they will and must find fault with him. Since consciousness steadily enlarges itself, in the absence of modifying factors, others will tend to find more fault with him while he gives them, as a parent, more reason for doing so.

At the same time, the part of his brain record pertinent to his being a teacher records the fact that he, in that capacity, is right. Simultaneously, however, he has excused himself by blaming the parents. Therefore, he will and must attract to himself reflections in the form of people and situations who give him excuses and, eventually, more reasons to make excuses.

We can readily see how complicated the situation could become in case our parent-teacher, in addition to blaming the parents for the *status quo*, should choose to do likewise for the teachers. This would establish in him a dual sense of right as a parent and as teacher, as well as a sense of wrong under both headings. The same pertains also to the excuses he has made. Consequently, he will tend to attract to himself acknowledgement (which reflects the right he related to himself as parent and teacher), blame (which reflects the wrong he related to himself as teacher and parent), and excuses (which reflect the excuses he made for himself as teacher as well as parent).

Acknowledgement may come from a principal, parent, mate, colleague, outsider, and sometimes from a pupil. Blame may originate from any of these human factors. The same holds true for excuses. They could come, with exasperating frequency, from pupils. They could also be given by a principal ("Sorry, but we couldn't award you the research grant you requested. There was no extra money available this year.") Or by others in more or less undesirable forms.

Obviously, children have no choice but to make excuses as long as their elders do likewise, whether they realize this fact or not. Here again is proof of unconscious communication by means of what we choose to call SSP (or suprasensory perception) rather than ESP. In addition, there is the transmittal, by means of the DNA, of ancestral habits of making excuses.

We are thus able to ascribe responsibility for excuse-making in children to two principal types of influences. One is hereditary or vertical. The other is contemporary or horizontal. Besides, there is a third type. It consists of excuses originating with the child. As a rule, these perpetuate the already established pattern and are merely individualized variations on the basic theme.

One major conclusion is inevitable. Unless adults — whether teachers, parents or others — refrain from making excuses, children will find it difficult if not impossible to stop emulating them. This is why scolding, offering rewards or similar devices usually fail to work.

Effects of Excuse-Making:

Another vital factor deserves consideration here. It pertains to a few generally overlooked effects excuse-making can have upon you and all who indulge in it. One is general, the other specific, in nature.

When you say, for instance, that you didn't do something because of what another person said, did or didn't do or because of an unexpected condition, you delegate the power over you and your affairs to a factor apparently beyond your control. To be sure, you didn't originate this undesirable trend. Your father may have taught you, orally or by the transmittal to you of the appropriate feelings and thoughts that the depression or sickness of his younger brother kept him from going to college.

Conversely, your mother may have implied that if it hadn't been for her mother's pleas she would never have married your father. Besides, you may have been told that your father's constant drinking prevented your mother from having the time required to give you the attention you wanted. Or that your mother's criticism kept your father from concentrating on his career, thus bringing about his failure.

The tenor of all this consciously and unconsciously transmitted information is helplessness on the part of your father and mother. Since half the chromosomes in each cell of your body came from your paternal ancestry while the other half originated with your mother's side, you cannot help but feel a sense of helplessness with regard to yourself. As a result, whether you are aware of this fact or not, you will tend to manufacture excuses to justify your not doing this or that.

Consequently, you will bring people and situations into your life which keep you from reaching your goals or achieving what would make you truly happy. Therefore, as long as you perpetuate the habit of making excuses, your faithful brain will manufacture the ways and means to create circumstances beyond your control which enable you to make more excuses. These may pertain to delay, sickness, accident, lack of time or money, litigation or the dishonesty or unreliability of others. Yet, you should remind yourself that all these undesirable events had to be established conceptually in your mind before their manifestation in tangible form. Therefore, they have no reality except the one you give them by what you feel, think or say. They can thus be removed by the same conceptual process that created them in the first place.

Master of Your Destiny:

When you no longer contend with delay, sickness, opposition, irresponsibility, and other nonsense (remember, the true nature of life is good and right), then you will stop being the victim of people or circumstances and become the master of your destiny. You will have eliminated excuses — and whatever they brought you in undeniably tangible form — from your life. As a result, you will prosper, unaffected by inflation or depression, be healthy in the midst of so-called epidemics, and happy because you know that, thanks to your enlightened new awareness, no person or situation can harm you.

Based on what we have said so far, we are sure you have grasped a vital point: *You are responsible for what you feel, think, say and do about yourself and others.*

By making excuses, you have given the responsibility for what happens to you to others. You have made yourself helpless and dependent upon other people and circumstances. You have done so with your own, though mostly unconscious, consent. You gave it. Therefore, you alone can revoke it. Do it now. Practice the art of assuming responsibility for everything that happens to you. Blame no one and nothing. Say: "Everything always happens exactly as I want it to happen," even when it may not be true initially. This will establish a pattern whereby in due course you will be pleased by the people and events in your life. Emulate as much as possible that splendid man from Missouri, President Harry S Truman, whose motto was, "The buck stops here!"

Let others see that strength and self-sufficiency are the rule in your life. Take a leaf out of little Janet's book. The daughter of one of our clients in the San Bernardino area, she suddenly vanished from her mother's sight during a shopping trip to a supermarket. The anxious woman had her paged. There was no answer. Finally, the tiny girl emerged from behind a stack of cereal boxes. Asked to explain her strange behavior, she had a ready answer: "I didn't want people to know that Janet was lost."

When you stop making excuses, your life will assume a new hue. You will become confident. Self-reliant. You will be on time. Dependable. Alert. Pleased with yourself.

12. ASSERT YOURSELF

A few years ago an artist named Steig became famous because his drawings spoke for millions. One of his most popular creations, reproduced on greeting cards, cocktail napkins and pillow cases, showed a smiling young lady, her voluptuous figure totally naked, whose right arm was gingerly draped around a lamp post while with her left hand she raised skyward a full glass of bubbly. "Public opinion no longer worries me," read the caption. It was written, please note, at a time when nudity was banned from the screen, a cause for arrest even in off-beat nightclubs, and frowned upon everywhere except, perhaps, nurseries.

To many, the happy nude was a symbol of assertiveness, protesting, no doubt, prolonged social repression from the cradle to the grave. In her own graphic way she obviously contributed to more recent developments that shattered age-old traditions. Her example enlarged the nationwide, if not worldwide, consciousness of protest against what was then the prevailing code. Typically, many women thought: "If she can do it, so can I." Like the majority of people, they were not assertive. They were merely copy-cats.

Most of us are afraid to assert ourselves. Like all human behavior, this has several reasons. The first, and probably most prevalent, is based on conscious or unconscious imitation of at least one parental model. This holds true even in cases where the individual was given up for adoption right after birth or doesn't even know the instigator of his restraint. We ascribe this phenomenon to genetic factors. (In our paper on Mental Genetics, we showed that only one-third of the cell nucleus or DNA contains biological data about our ancestors. The rest is based upon information pertaining to ancestral personality factors, attitudes, and patterns of behavior and experience.)

Conditioning:

The second reason is conditioning. During preceding incidents, the individual learned to keep quiet in response to the dictum of parents, grandparents, teachers, ministers and other elders to the effect that children should be seen but not heard and other platitudes. Although he may now be 20 or 90, his brain-recorded learning still forces him to be silent. He will rationalize this in terms that are perfectly plausible to him by telling himself, even though the opposite may be true, that people will shame, misunderstand or dislike him or see that he is wrong.

Speak Up:

A third and quite common reason for non-assertion is the belief that by speaking up, he'll hurt others, start an argument or be seen as a trouble-maker. As a rule, nothing could be further from the truth. By being silent, he actually tells other people that he acquiesces to their neglect, insult or trespass against his rights. Besides, he gives implied consent to more undesirable behavior along these lines, by the culprit as well as others. It doesn't matter whether they know or don't know of his passivity. His unconscious communication system impels them to act along the offensive lines. "Go ahead," he signals them, "step on me again." Or: "Ask me for money, time or services without repayment or other form of compensation." When they do, he and others will condemn them without realizing his contributory role to the transgression.

If he learns to follow our advice, he won't wait until the resulting irritation accumulates, incident upon incident, into anger that eventually could get completely out of hand. Instead, he will speak up, as calmly and reasonably as possible, on every occasion that presents itself. Thereby, he will serve notice on relatives, friends, associates, and all he deals with — but, most of all, himself — that he is through being delayed, lied to, used or manipulated. Provided he remains firm and, if need be, terminates relations with the trespassers, his newly established resoluteness will win respect for him from himself and others — not to mention their eventual cooperation.

By refusing to deal with offenders against his rights — including relatives, professionals, businessmen, employees and servants — he secures for himself the tranquility and freedom from irritation that are the reward of those who, to paraphrase Patrick Henry, are eternally vigilant.

What is true for international relations applies equally on an interpersonal basis. The result of such constant, impartial alertness benefits and profits, in the long run, the assertive individual and all who are involved with him. For he as well as they learn to function by rules that are fair and equitable. In turn, these rules will enrich the lives of many who may never suspect, let alone meet, their actual benefactors. This truth proves again that we all are centers of influence, and everything we do or don't do is meaningful. The rules by which we live are more important than the money we may leave to our heirs. The former are a permanent legacy, safe from arbitrary repeal. A monetary inheritance, on the other hand, may vanish because of inflation, legal manipulation, a feud among heirs, or waste.

As long as you don't let the person you love or deal with know where you stand, he is free to assume that whatever he does or doesn't do is all right with you.

When you fail to demand time and time again that you get your steak exactly the way you ordered it in a restaurant, you open the door to eventually missing out on the contract, promotion or social advantage you want.

By habitually ignoring your spouse's, friend's or laundryman's delay, you may slow your rate of progress in life.

Example of Self-Assertion:

Cindy, a young lady client of ours, had dated Mike, a charming executive, for years. Although he was undependable, stingy, sometimes downright rude to her, in addition to going out with other women, she remained patient and silent. By continuing to grant him the favors he seemed to demand from her, we showed her that she actually rewarded him for his wrongdoing.

A chronic stomach disorder indicated her anxiety over and resentment of his erratic behavior. Visits to several physicians failed to give her relief. We established a comprehensive and consistent improvement program for her. At first, understandably, she was reluctant to lay down rules for her male friend.

Her mother, she recalled, had not asserted herself toward her father, and the few times she opened her mouth resulted in violent fights. Cindy, under our direction, learned to speak to Mike with calm logic. He responded well. In fact, he was so smitten by her explanations that he soon foresook, as the saying goes, all others and asked her to marry him, an unprecedented move for a supposedly perennial bachelor. Remember, when you say no to wrong, you say yes to what is right!

From Repression to Expression:

We have found that sometimes people who have repressed anger most of their lives become irrational or violent when learning to speak up. Don't let this scare you. When the pendulum of life swings from repression to expression, we should not be surprised at such a development. After the cumulative resentment, first harbored against a parent, sibling, playmate, and, later, others, has run its course, the individual is free to express his or her feelings in a progressively calmer and more rational manner. Occasional outbursts cannot harm you or others. Remember Mother Nature. The most fertile soil on this planet is lava, by-product of volcanic eruptions. By analogy, in human relations, the greatest progress often occurs after similar explosions. We are sure you can provide your own first-hand examples.

Many well-meaning ministers and teachers of etiquette favor repression. They say: "Good Christians" — or Jews, Buddhists, Muslims, or whatever religion you may follow — "should always be serene." "Well-bred ladies" — or gentlemen or young people — "don't raise their voices." This advice disregards the example of nature. There are four seasons — not just Spring, usually depicted as sunny and peaceful. You are a miniature earth — with the gamut of emotions dormant within you. So, don't feel bad or guilty when people sometimes liken you to lightning, thunder or a tornado.

Occasional explosions, if based upon a thorough understanding of the underlying dynamics, may save your life. Direct expression certainly is preferable to its behavioral counterpart: indirect expression. It merely is a constant which has many variable modifications, such as alcoholism, over-eating, gambling, compulsive buying, criminality or sickness in the form of ulcers, cancer or other conditions (see Fig. 4). In time, direct expression may serve to make unnecessary the need for excessive assertiveness. As a result, everyone will give you more and more cooperation.

When you hold your anger inside, you may liken yourself to a boiler filled with steam. With your unconscious radar scanning device you are in search of a safety valve — a person honest enough to explode for you before you burst. Many a spouse, employee, friend and even stranger has been divorced, fired, cursed or sued for serving as the unwitting mouthpiece of the very one or ones who piously condemned them.

Remember, you are not out to win a popularity contest. At least, not with others. The most important thing, especially during this vital retraining period, is that you like yourself. In the long run, we are sure, your new and assertive self will please you much more than your formerly submissive *alter ego*. The latter state no doubt earned you frustration if not contempt. Assertiveness, however, cannot help but make you truly satisfied and effective.

Be Heard:

Mankind is a huge, well-balanced chorus. By refusing to let your voice be heard, you are copping out. You deprive the whole of the benefit of your contribution.

Years ago, we proved that it is possible to accomplish on a citywide scale what we do in private consultations, seminars and lectures: teach people to assert themselves in a constructive manner. In a series of hour-long television and radio programs hosted by our good friend, Owen Spann*, we taught many San Franciscans and Northern Californians how to get parking spaces, choice seats and service in restaurants, promotions, proposals and other benefits. Their

*over KPIX-TV and KGO, 1968-1971.

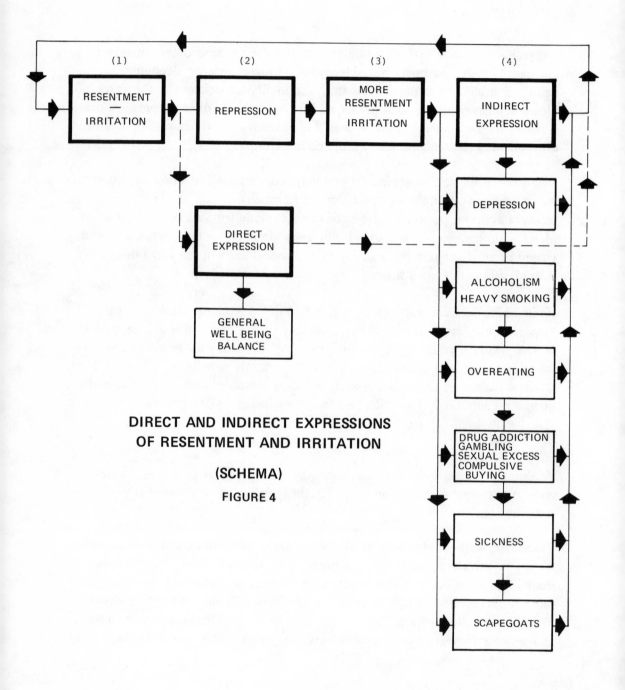

**DIRECT AND INDIRECT EXPRESSIONS
OF RESENTMENT AND IRRITATION**

(SCHEMA)

FIGURE 4

letters furnish ample proof that they were satisfied with the results.

The meek, we are told, shall inherit the earth, trouble and all. Therefore, we long ago concluded that only the bold enter into heaven with all its glories. That's why we are so emphatic. You'd better learn to be, if necessary, mad and expressive, although public opinion may crucify you, rather than maudlin and repressed.

13. WATCH WHAT YOU HEAR

If you are like most people nowadays, you probably know all about diet. You may watch what you eat with the utmost care. You wouldn't dare put more than so many calories in your mouth per day. Let alone candy, cholesterol or whatever else scientists may be saying isn't good for you.

In stark contrast, unless you happen to be the rare exception to the rule, you probably are downright negligent when it comes to listening to others. In this aspect, you probably are like your garbage disposal unit. Anything and everything goes in. Your mother may have taught you that it's the height of rudeness to ignore what Aunt Amalia says or to change the subject when a neighbor complains about her husband's drinking or snoring. As a result, you have been conditioned to sit, listen and suffer while pretending you liked it.

You don't have to be a physician to diagnose your mate's, child's, friend's or your own case of indigestion. He, she or you ate too much. Or partook of the wrong type of food. The same holds true for the symptoms of depression, a condition that seems to have reached endemic — if not epidemic — proportions in this supposedly advanced age. As a rule, we have found, it's misnamed. It actually is repression. Repression of anger or the impulse to lash out at those who impose upon you their troubles. Who fill your ears — and therefore also your brain — with bad news. In effect, they are trying to sell you on the idea that they, their family, their business and the world are in a mess.

If they are unreasonable in imposing their laments upon you, so, dear friend and reader, are you, whether as the result of hereditary, contemporary or circumstantial factors, in letting them rob you of your peace of mind. Here is another case of implied consent. Your doctor may prescribe uppers or other anti-depressants for you. A second physician may suggest shock treatments. A third may tell you to take a cruise to get away from it all. A fourth may just listen and commiserate. None of this will help. For, unless you rise up in rebellion against those trespassers, you will attract them again and again, whether you are at home, in a sanatorium or on a luxury liner. The faces may change. And the exact nature of the woes. But the effect upon you will remain the same.

Example:

Martin, one of our clients, a dynamic actor, had an excellent marriage. He and his wife, Kim, usually were a happy team. Once, after returning from location in Utah, they had a fight that threatened to sever their union permanently. We found that Martin, while away from home, had permitted a few fellow actors to sell him on the idea that their spouses, girlfriends and other women had betrayed or abused them. Repetitive exposure to these tales eventually caused him to identify with the complainants. It reinforced his righteous indignation against the offending females. By the time he reached home, he had mentally become the one who, with a fury rooted in love, would avenge the wrongs inflicted upon his seemingly innocent friends. Just as he made himself the singular symbol of revenge for many, so he, unconsciously to be sure, selected Kim as the singular target to subdue in payment for the sins, real or imaginary, of the women who had wronged his friends.

By the rules of mind, as we discovered and use them, beautiful Kim, though geographically apart from him, had joined him in thought, feeling and action. As his perfect counterpart, she, though unaware of his role as listener to the complaints of other males, began to play a role paralleling his. Only those who filled her ears with their laments were the very females Martin had learned to see as tramps and gold-diggers. As a result, she began to regard her husband's cohorts as chasers, tightwads, and cowards. By the time the formerly happy couple got together, Kim had become the spokeswomen for her fellow sisters in neglect, hurling against the equally furious Martin the epithets that the others had been too repressed to utter. At the same time, he expressed toward her the grudges secretly harbored by his drinking buddies. A perfect example of the reflection principle in action!

We showed these fine people the reason for their feud. They readily saw that they both had served as scapegoats for others too inarticulate or fearful to call a spade a spade. From now on, they resolved, they'd let others do their own talking and fight their own battles. Most of all, they wouldn't listen to the complaints of other people.

Screen Your Input:

There is a profound lesson in this. If you wish to get — or remain — married, associate only with happy couples. Shun those who continuously quarrel or berate each other behind their backs. In case you yearn for success, turn your mental hearing aid off as soon as someone says that the country is going to the dogs . . . the President, Congress, Big Business or the unions are wrecking the economy . . . no one can hope to make it with today's tax structure.

Whether you dream of getting a degree, marketing an invention or seeing the world, remember that there will always be those who think they are benefiting you by telling you that you are wasting your time. That you'd better think small and prepare for the worst.

As a matter of fact, they are doing you a favor. They are reminding you that you are on the right track. That you are in very good company. Because that's what their contemporaries said to, and about, the Fultons, the Edisons, the Wrights.

Don't Listen to Negative Advice:

It matters little what people say to you. What *does* matter is what you record in your brain. So thank them aloud for their concern but silently tell yourself that you will and must succeed just as those who preceded you have and as you no doubt did on previous occasions. You may have made the high-school football team against your parents' expectations or been asked to the senior prom when you — and everybody else — feared you'd have to watch television at home. Or gotten through algebra, despite your teacher's predictions of disaster.

Your continued and determined effort in the direction of your goal speaks louder than all the words of others and your own previous doubts.

In dealing with complainers, perhaps you will benefit from another example of one of our clients. Every day she drove her car to her office with three neighbors who paid the expenses. But these women shared another habit which was most offensive to our client. They constantly complained about their mates, children, mothers, mothers-in-law, health and other conditions. Without losing them as riders, she wished to get them on a more positive track. We proposed that she tell them that she was on the Teutsches' "Good News Diet." Therefore, she could only listen to what was right, good and pleasant. Anyone breaking the diet rules, would have to put a dollar in her kitty. The riders laughed but agreed that, perhaps, she had a good idea. The first day she collected seven dollars. The next day four. In less than a week, the members of this car pool were reporting only good news about their families and themselves. All frowns and headaches had disappeared.

Remember, you are the publisher, editor, reporter and subject of a daily lifelong journal. Whatever you put into the headlines, whether it's about yourself or others, will reproduce itself in the form of more and more news along the established line. Such black-bordered editions as "Joe is Broke" or

"Mary is Sick" are the result not of an adverse fate but word patterns or a sloppy interpretation of the facts. In case you decided to announce that Joe had at least a hundred dollars or Mary felt better and better, your subconscious would soon enable you to announce progressively more cheerful news about yourself.

Remember another vital fact: *What you think or say about others eventually will and must pertain to you.*

Gene Tunney practiced what we preach here. The press heavily favored Jack Dempsey, the fearsome Manassa Mauler, to win the "Bout of the Century." Tunney banished all newspaper reporters from his training camp. When he entered the ring against the up-to-then undefeated Dempsey, he was in a mind free of doubt or fear. He became heavyweight champion of the world in one of boxing's greatest upsets.

Guard Your Mental Threshold:

As you guard the threshold of your mental house, you will refuse admittance to words of discouragement, whether from friends, strangers or the news media. You either must ignore them, prove them wrong or tell yourself, "This can't happen to me or those I love."

That's a mental diet you can't buy, even in a healthfood store. Yet, it is guaranteed to avoid depression and its inevitable effects upon your body and affairs.

14. BE PATIENT

Many people have not learned to be patient. In this way, they handicap themselves unnecessarily. They are controlled by the belief that others or circumstances keep them from attaining what they want or that an expected event may take place too late for them to benefit. In this manner, of course, they merely create more obstacles and delays for themselves.

Mental law decrees that every action or impatience directed against others must return to us in due course. You already know from what we have said that the target of our impatience need not be the one repaying us.

Every time we feel impatient with the driver of a car ahead of us, we may set the stage for a future experience in which a prospect is impatient with us, cutting us short in midst of our presentation, or in which our spouse refuses to understand us.

This clearly illustrates the need for patience. Our impatience with others, as well as our resentment against those who are impatient with us, may be due to our failure to understand them and the cause of their behavior.

Equally, if not more important, is the requirement that you be patient with yourself. Remember, your consciousness was shaped some time ago. The new habit or belief you are trying to cultivate is like a baby. Precisely as this little tyke would be discouraged when scolded for not walking or talking like an adult, so the new way of life inside you needs patience, practice, and encouragement.

Although you have planted new seeds, for a while you will continue to reap the results of your previous beliefs and actions. Your fear of an accident, theft, argument, though hidden beneath the threshold of awareness, may still cause a corresponding experience. Instead of being despondent at that time, be glad when this happens. For in the physical event your subconscious belief is expressed and discarded forever, provided you don't let yourself be fooled into being upset, discouraged or fearful. Remind yourself that better days lie ahead.

Be like a farmer after planting time. He would not dig up the new seeds to see if they are growing. Instead, he cultivates and irrigates the soil, leaving the rest up to nature.

In the process of acquiring a new consciousness it is well to remember that your earliest learning has made the deepest impression in your brain record. Therefore, you will become consciously aware of it at the very end of your efforts to change, just as oldtimers will clearly recall episodes from their earliest years. Your more recently acquired beliefs and experiences are either above or only slightly below the layer separating conscious from subconscious awareness. Your relations with outsiders will improve first, while you and your mate may continue to quarrel for a while. For both of you are reflecting each other's deep-seated resentments of long ago that probably originated in association with your parents or others close to you.

At times you may still be unhappy with your job, finances, or marriage. Don't give up. Reason with yourself. Think of the growing process that is taking place within you. A baby does not become an adult overnight. It takes a seed several years to grow into a tree. And, then, remember this. Midnight is the darkest portion of the night. Yet one second later, the new day has started. Soon you will see the dawn.

Compare yourself to the pupa inside a cocoon. It would like very much to be a butterfly. But it cannot struggle free until it has gained all the nourishment, strength, and growth necessary for adulthood. Liberated even one second ahead of its time, it would die.

It took all your experiences, all the people, all the ups and downs in your life, including your mistakes, to produce into being your present self. Whoever you are, whatever you do, wherever you may be at this moment, you have gathered and are gathering unto yourself at all times the ingredients necessary for your attainment of the butterfly stage.

Believe in Yourself:

Believe in your family, your occupation, yourself. Realize the goodness, the beauty, the glorious meaning of life. Most of all, trust the spirit or superintelligence within you that is mightier even than the subconscious. Through your yearnings and frustrations it is directing you at all times to the people, places, and situations required for your progress. In everything that happens to you, even in reading these pages, you are being led to an ever more beneficial use of your thoughts, feelings, words, and actions. In this manner, your former apparent enemy, the subconscious, will become your friend. Your fear will be converted into confidence, failure into success, hate into love, lack into fulfillment and abundance, misery into happiness.

And what holds true for you applies also to the beggar in the street, the millionaire, the student, the ditchdigger, the statesman, be he American, Spanish, Japanese, or Russian.

Knowing this, you can be patient. As you do each day the best you know how, you will become understanding and confident as never before. The more confident you are, the better you will do, and the more confidence others will have in you.

Cheer Up:

Like the pendulum of a clock or the ocean wave, life pulsates from one extreme to another. If you have been miserable, defeated, despondent so far, cheer up. Change is the only constant there is. It took you a few decades to become the person you are. Fortunately, a much shorter time will be required to convert you into your new and greater self. Here is why:

a. Abundance, goodness, achievements, and well-being are natural for you and all creation. We merely have been taught otherwise.

b. You know now exactly how to proceed to raise your consciousness to any level you may desire. Actually, since you are returning to what is natural for you, this will be easy.

Don't envy others. Otherwise, you create more reasons for envy. Friends may have more money than you, but perhaps you have greater wisdom, peace of mind, capability, freedom. Someone else may seem to be more intelligent than you. You, on the other hand, have a more pleasing personality. Life is just. Wherein we lack, another has abundance. In whatever we are well supplied, he is poor.

Don't pity others. For this way you decree that you will be pitied sooner or later. Know that the object of your feeling is, like you, in a state required for his progress. Every man you meet is either as you are, were, or will be.

To our reasoning intelligence we may differ. Actually, though, we all are part and parcel of the same magnificent whole. Separation exists in one place only: our concept.

You may wonder at the seemingly erratic course of your life. But the following considerations should put you at ease.

The tiniest particle of the smallest atom in your body moves with the same amazing predictability that governs the revolution of the planets around the sun and of solar systems in intergalactic space. If the smallest as well as the largest bodies in our universe thus are in constant lawful and orderly motion, one conclusion is inevitable. Man, as an intermediate component of the cosmos, must also move in the same lawful manner, although to the uninformed eye this may not be apparent. In some of our examples we have shown that even what we call an accident is governed by mental law.

Therefore, dear friend, rest assured. You are at the right place at the right time, doing the right thing.

By following our suggestions, you will raise your consciousness day by day. Your new state of mind will free you of your former false beliefs and fears. Everyone and everything will benefit you. People must conform to your knowledge of their goodness. You may lose your position, money, opportunity. But your subconscious fulfillment and security will attract to you an even better position, even more money, an even greater opportunity through any of an infinite number of channels.

No matter how wide the gap between your present state and the happier future of which you dream, what we have told you will help you bridge it. With persistent effort, you cannot fail.

B. SUMMARY

And now some words about happiness. To us, it is one of man's natural states. Yes, we all have an inborn sense of happiness. Obviously, Thomas Jefferson and the other Founding Fathers knew this, or they would not have equated the right to its pursuit with the right to life and liberty.

Don't judge from your present perspective. Just watch a baby humming to itself, a little boy with his puppy, a group of youngsters at play. Remember when you received your first kiss — or bicycle, or car?

If this is so, you may ask, then where do all those unhappy people come from?

We'd like to remind you that their attitude — and resulting experiences — are determined by three crucial factors.

One is their hereditary predisposition. If their grandparents or parents were disgruntled people, they can't be blamed for following in their footsteps.

The second factor is environmental imposition. It takes place in the form of sayings by so-called authorities such as: "Life isn't a bed of roses," "Only idiots are happy," or, "How can you be happy when so many people are miserable?"

The third is your own personal interpretation of the preceding causes, coupled with your own personal behavior and experiences.

Interpretation:

The key word is "interpretation." Just as you can look at a glass of water and call it either half full or half empty, so it is with every situation in your life. You have the right to tag it anything you wish — excellent, so-so, or hopeless. Each label has its own unique way of affecting you. The same holds true for people. You may regard them as friends, stimulants, bores, irritants or foes. You'll soon see your judgment has come true for you. Another person, more optimistic or pessimistic than you, will get his own, totally different, but totally predictable result.

Remember, you are not your gloomy grandpa on your dad's side. Neither are you your careworn mother or tearful, sickly aunt. You are you. A happy you. A worried you. An in-between you. Yours is the choice.

This is the gist of our message. Because you now know the truth, you are not a robot, mechanically imitating this or that human model. You can cease being a copy-cat. You can start a new step-by-step self improvement program today.

Practice Confidence:

Practice being confident. Start by reminding yourself of all the skills you already have mastered — and if it's only walking, talking and winning at poker. You are not helpless. You have it within your reach to cope with any person or situation. Practice thinking, feeling and speaking about him, her or it the right way.

Practice making yourself aware of what pleases you about yourself and others. Increase your sense of enjoyment second by second, minute by minute, hour by hour, day by day.

Don't compare yourself to others. They had different elders and conditioning than you. Analyze the dicta, right or wrong, imposed upon you by your parents or others. Do you still live by them? Or have you modified them in accordance with your needs?

Don't let others impose their standards or wishes upon you. Neither impose yours upon them. For this is the tyranny of the mind condemned by Thomas Jefferson and all righteous thinkers. It can, will and must backfire upon the tyrant. If you wish to be free, give all those you know the freedom to be themselves.

Don't wait for a contingency. Many people do. They think they can't be happy until they live in a certain house, drive a certain car, wear certain clothes, marry a certain type, or have a particular kind of education or job. Others think they must be a certain age, height or weight, have a certain bank balance or, like one of our business clients, have a pushbutton phone on their desk. If you are dissatisfied now, you'll be more dissatisfied tomorrow. That's one of the rules of the subconscious.

Practice Happiness:

Practice being happy — right now. With yourself. With your looks. With your family, your mate, your parents, your children, and even your dog. With your talents, your boss, your associates, your employees. Make whatever improvements you can or wish. Accept the rest. Like it, or, at least, try to learn to like it.

Use what you now know about life to your advantage. Fight the tendency to revert to doubt, fear or depression. Join happy people, do happy things, think happy thoughts.

Make light of things. Don't take yourself — or others — so seriously. Have a good laugh now and then. Don't worry about how well you may follow our advice. Learn by doing. It should be fun — not a struggle. Be happy with everything you have done or experienced so far.

Don't let the challenges confronting you rob you of your confidence and serenity. Compare yourself to the baby chick. Neither the mother hen nor the human hand can help it peck through the egg's shell. It has been given the strength and intelligence required for survival. But it must use and develop them to peck through. The same holds true for you. You've got what it takes to deal with any contingency.

Don't live in remorse or regret. Everything you did, no matter how much you may condemn it now, was necessary to make you the person you are today. Every person you knew — or know, every experience you had — or have, every situation confronting you then — or now, was — and is — necessary to give you the competence and wisdom you enjoy today. Life is a 100-meter race. You couldn't start it on the finish line. You had to pass, meter by meter, through the involvements and experiences that bring you closer to your goal.

Be grateful for what you are, what you have and what you know. You are luckier than you think.

Express Appreciation:

Every day, give happiness to others. Don't give to them in accordance with what you think they should have. Give to them what makes them happy. In case of doubt, don't give to them what you want or what they want — but rather what is right. Give whatever you can. Even if it's only a smile, a word of encouragement, a sign that you care. Watch how quickly you will be rewarded. By a sense of pleasure, by appreciation from the one to whom you gave whatever you could. In case you should not receive the reciprocation you expect, the fault may not lie with the other one but with your sense of not being appreciated. Remedy this. Express appreciation. Direct your attention to all the people who gave you appreciation. The other person isn't your father, mother or sister who may have rejected you.

Don't cater to weakness, to hopelessness, to wrong. Wrong contains within it its own self-destruct mechanism. It has only short-term duration. Concentrate not on what has happened to you or another but rather on the thoughts, words, deeds or misdeeds that brought it about. Be happy that justice rules the universe. For it relentlessly metes out rewards for wrong. By the same token, even greater are its rewards for right. Don't blame others for what they do or say to you but look for the contributory cause within yourself. Demand the best from yourself and others. Give the best in return.

Persevere:

Persist. In due course, you will acquire a growing sense of satisfaction. One day it will become a pattern. You will have learned what probably is the most important habit on earth: the happiness habit.

The public and private schools teach the three r's, mathematics, geography, history, English and foreign languages. But, as yet, they don't teach the subject matter set forth by us which includes the steps to happiness. That's why, regardless of how many degrees you hold, you are not truly educated until you master the essence of what we have written.

Don't look back or yearn for the good old days. You weren't as knowledgeable then or skillful. Neither would you — or we — live without electric light or appliances, air conditioning or subsonic as well as supersonic flight.

Today is a glorious day of opportunity for you. To put our advice into practice, do something that makes you feel good. It takes know-how and effort to rewire the printed circuit of ancestral habit imbedded in your brain even before you were born. It takes discipline in thought, word and action, in this age of temptation and self-indulgence, to be true to one's resolve and to those involved in marriage, career and other relationships. This moment, and from now on, reach higher and higher toward the greater you which is beckoning. Practice excelling in whatever you do.

Going through what it takes to reach your goal may not always be pleasant. Compare it to a course required for graduation from school. Therefore, accept it. Like it. Don't lose sight of the end result.

As you become the greater *you* you were meant to be, a new sense of pleasure will suffuse you.

That is the harbinger of true happiness.